# HOLT

# Chemistry

S0-BAV-300

## Study Guide

**HOLT, RINEHART AND WINSTON**

A Harcourt Education Company

Orlando • **Austin** • New York • San Diego • Toronto • London

ISBN 0-03-066742-9

12  13  14  15  862  09  08  07

# Contents

Skills Worksheet )

# Concept Review

## Section: What Is Chemistry?

**Complete each statement below by underlining the correct word or phrase in brackets.**

1. A chemical is any substance that has [definite, indefinite] composition. Changes in chemicals, or chemical reactions, take place [only in test tubes, all around us].

2. The type and arrangement of [particles, crystals] in a sample of matter determine the properties of the matter. Most of the matter you encounter is in one of [numerous, three] states of matter.

3. The characteristics of a solid include [fixed, variable] volume and shape. Particles that make up solids are held [loosely, tightly] in a [flexible, rigid] structure, so the particles can [vibrate only slightly, flow past each other].

4. Liquids have a [fixed, variable] volume but a [fixed, variable] shape. This situation occurs because particles in a liquid are held [tightly, loosely] and [can, cannot] slip past each other.

5. Gases have [fixed, variable] volume and [fixed, variable] shape. Gas particles may move apart to fill any container they occupy. This behavior occurs because gas particles are [close together, far apart] and are [attracted, not stongly attracted] to one another.

6. [Physical, Chemical] changes are changes in which the identity of a substance does not change. Thus the changes of state are [physical, chemical] changes.

7. In a [physical, chemical] change, the identities of substances change and new substances form.

8. In the word equation *hydrogen + oxygen + heat → water*, hydrogen is a [reactant, product], and water is a [reactant, product]. This is an example of a [physical, chemical] change.

9. A [physical, chemical] reaction rearranges the atoms that make up the reactant or reactants. After a chemical reaction, [the same, different] atoms are present in the product or products. Atoms [are, are not] destroyed or created, so mass [does, does not] change during a chemical reaction.

10. Chemical changes sometimes produce a gas, which you can detect by observing [bubbles, a precipitate] or by a change in [color, odor].

11. When two clear solutions mix and a precipitate forms, the mixture becomes [clear, cloudy].

12. When energy is released during a chemical reaction, temperature [increases, decreases]. Chemical reactions may also absorb energy, which is indicated by a(n) [increase, decrease] in temperature.

13. A color change in a reaction system, such as when an indicator changes color, may indicate that a [chemical, physical] reaction has occurred and [new, no new] substances have formed.

Name _____ Class _____ Date _____

**| Concept Review** *continued*

**Mark each change below *P* if it is physical and *C* if it is chemical.**

_____ **14.** milk souring

_____ **15.** gasoline burning

_____ **16.** ice melting

_____ **17.** lighting a match

_____ **18.** water evaporating

_____ **19.** chopping wood

_____ **20.** burning wood

_____ **21.** breath fogging a mirror

_____ **22.** cooking an egg

_____ **23.** bleaching a stain

**Answer the following questions in the space provided.**

**24.** Explain how chemicals and chemical reactions are an important part of your life.

_____

_____

_____

**25.** In the spaces below draw and label a microscopic view showing the particles in a solid, a liquid, and a gas.

Skills Worksheet

# Concept Review

## Section: Describing Matter

**Answer the following questions in the space provided.**

1. Describe two characteristic properties of matter.

_____

_____

2. Briefly explain the difference between mass and weight.

_____

_____

3. Briefly explain the difference between quantity and unit.

_____

_____

4. Briefly explain why density is a derived unit.

_____

_____

5. What special meaning does the slope of a graph of mass versus volume have?

_____

6. List three examples of physical change and three examples of chemical change.

_____

_____

_____

7. What are the differences between physical and chemical properties? Give an example of a chemical property.

_____

_____

_____

_____

| Concept Review *continued*

For each statement that is true, write T in the blank next to the item number. For each statement that is false, write F in the blank next to the item number and corrrect the underlined word to make the statement correct.

_____ **8.** The terms *odorless* and *colorless* are <u>quantitative</u> terms.

_____

_____ **9.** To say that the mass of a gold nugget is 5.0 grams is to use a <u>quantitative</u> term.

_____

_____ **10.** The <u>kelvin</u> is used to express length in SI.

_____

_____ **11.** The <u>pound</u> is used to express forces such as weight in SI.

_____

_____ **12.** The <u>liter</u> is used to express volume in SI.

_____

**Solve the following problems, and write your answer in the space provided.**

**13.** How many millimeters are there in 2.0 meters?

**14.** How many grams are there in 5.0 kilograms?

# Concept Review

## Section: How is Matter Classified?

**Write the name of the element for each chemical symbol listed below.**

**1.** C _____

**2.** S _____

**3.** N _____

**4.** Au _____

**5.** Hg _____

**6.** Sn _____

**Write the symbol of each element listed below.**

_____ **7.** silver

_____ **8.** lead

_____ **9.** potassium

_____ **10.** iron

_____ **11.** sodium

_____ **12.** copper

**Write the answer to the following questions in the space provided.**

**13.** How does an atom differ from an element?

_____

**14.** How does an atom differ from a molecule?

_____

_____

**15.** What is an allotrope?

_____

_____

Name _____ Class _____ Date _____

**Concept Review** *continued*

**16.** When is a sample of matter considered a pure substance?

_____

_____

**17.** What is the difference between a mixture and a compound?

_____

_____

_____

**18.** Briefly explain why a beaker containing sand and water is a mixture although sand itself is a pure substance.

_____

_____

_____

**19.** Briefly explain why a compound has characteristic properties.

_____

_____

**Label whether each material below is a pure substance, a homogeneous mixture, or a heterogeneous mixture.**

**20.** $C_2H_2$ _____

**21.** Au _____

**22.** Hg _____

**23.** $CH_3COOH$ _____

**24.** carbonated beverage _____

**25.** raisin bran cereal _____

**26.** stainless steel _____

**27.** $H_2O_2$ _____

**28.** orange juice _____

**29.** sugar _____

**30.** gasoline _____

# Concept Review

## Section: Energy

**Complete each statement below by writing the correct term in the space provided.**

**1.** The capacity to do work is _____.

**2.** A change in matter from one form to another without a change in chemical

properties is a _____ change.

**3.** A change that occurs when one or more substances change into new

substances with different properties is a _____ change.

**4.** A change in matter in which energy is absorbed is a(n) _____
process.

**5.** A change in matter in which energy is released is a(n) _____
process.

**6.** Energy must be added to a solid to melt it. This addition gives the particles

_____ energy, allowing them to move out of the crystalline

structure.

**7.** To freeze a substance, energy must be _____ from the substance.

**Write the answers to the following questions in the space provided.**

**8.** State the law of conservation of energy.

_____

_____

**9.** What is heat?

_____

_____

**10.** Define temperature.

_____

_____

Name _____  Class _____  Date _____

**Concept Review** *continued*

**11.** What is the difference between temperature and heat?

_____

_____

_____

**12.** Convert the following temperatures as indicated.

    **a.** 100°C = _____ K

    **b.** 293.15 K = _____ °C

    **c.** 55°C = _____ K

    **d.** 459 K = _____ °C

    **e.** 3 K = _____ °C

    **f.** −39°C = _____ K

**13.** Define specific heat.

_____

_____

_____

**14.** Substance A has a specific heat of 0.650 J/g·K, and substance B has a specific heat of 0.325 J/g·K. If 100 J of energy is applied to a 10 g sample of each substance, which substance will have a higher temperature? Why?

_____

_____

_____

_____

_____

Skills Worksheet

# Concept Review

## Section: Studying Matter and Energy

**Answer the following questions in the space provided.**

**1.** What are the fundamental procedures in the scientific method?

_____

_____

_____

**2.** Why is it important to publish the results of research findings?

_____

_____

_____

**3.** When performing an experiment, why is it important to have a control?

_____

_____

_____

**4.** What is a variable?

_____

_____

_____

**5.** What is the definition of a model?

_____

_____

_____

**6.** Why are models useful in chemistry?

_____

_____

_____

**In the space provided at the left of each word or phrase, write the letter of the expression on the right that is most closely related.**

_____ **7.** hypothesis

**a.** a well-tested explanation for a phenomenon based on observation, experimentation, and reasoning

_____ **8.** theory

**b.** a reasonable and testable explanation of observations

_____ **9.** scientific law

**c.** The products of a chemical reaction have the same mass as the reactants.

_____ **10.** law of conservation of mass

**d.** a description of the natural world that has been proven reliable over time

Skills Worksheet

# Concept Review

## Section: Measurements and Calculations in Chemistry

**Answer the following questions in the space provided.**

**1.** What is the difference between accuracy and precision?

_____

_____

**2.** Suppose a chemistry student took the mass of a sample of calcium carbonate and obtained the following values: 1.01 g, 1.00 g, 0.99 g, 0.98 g. The known mass was 1.00 g. Was this measurement accurate or precise? Explain your answer.

_____

_____

**3.** Determine the number of significant figures in the following.

_____ **a.** 4 001.006 g        _____ **f.** 10.000 004 56 g

_____ **b.** 3 cars        _____ **g.** 2000 000 g

_____ **c.** 0.000 0456 g        _____ **h.** 2000 000.0 g

_____ **d.** 1 001.000 000 g        _____ **i.** 2000 000 000.00 g

_____ **e.** 100 g        _____ **j.** 20 students

**4.** Explain why some numerical values have an unlimited number of significant digits.

_____

_____

_____

**Concept Review** *continued*

## Solve the following problems, and write your answer in the space provided.

**5.** Perform the following operations. Express your answers with the correct number of significant figures.

**a.** 37.26 m + 2.7 m + 0.0015 m = _____

**b.** 256.3 mL + 2 L + 137 mL + 10 L = _____

**c.** 300. kPa $\times$ 274.57 mL / 547 kPa = _____

**d.** 346 mL $\times$ 200 K / 546.4 K = _____

**6.** Convert the following to scientific notation.

**a.** 0.000 003 6 mm _____

**b.** 1 450 000 mg _____

**c.** 2340 m _____

**d.** 111.34 g/cm$^3$ _____

**7.** Perform the following calculations. Express your answers in scientific notation.

**a.** $4.5 \times 10^6 + 3.9 \times 10^8$ = _____

**b.** $(3.9 \times 10^3)(6.7 \times 10^2)$ = _____

**c.** $3.01 \times 10^{23} / 2.56 \times 10^6$ = _____

**d.** $5.6 \times 10^7 - 2.3 \times 10^6$ = _____

**e.** $6.7 \times 10^{12} + 7.8 \times 10^{12}$ = _____

**f.** $3.7 \times 10^{12} - 2.1 \times 10^{12}$ = _____

**g.** $(6.02 \times 10^{23})(2.00)$ = _____

**h.** $6.02 \times 10^{23} / 3.00$ = _____

**8.** Three chemistry students measured the length of a copper bar. The recorded lengths were 5.05 cm, 5 cm, and 5.1 cm. What is the average length of the bar?

**Concept Review** *continued*

9. Find the volume of a cube of zinc with the following dimensions: 3.000 cm, 3.1 cm, 2.99 cm.

10. Find the density in $g/cm^3$ of a rectangular prism with dimensions of $6.00 \times 10^2$ mm, $1.57 \times 10^3$ mm, 3147 mm and a mass of $6.02 \times 10^6$ g.

11. Find the average volume from the following volume readings: 3.00 mL, 2.0 mL, 2.987 mL, and 3.4856 mL.

Skills Worksheet

# Concept Review

## Section: Substances Are Made of Atoms

**In the blank at the left of each word or phrase, write the letter of the expression on the right that is most closely related.**

_____ **1.** atomic theory

**a.** This states that a chemical compound always contains the same elements in exactly the same proportions by weight or mass.

_____ **2.** law of definite proportions

**b.** This states that atoms are the building blocks of all matter.

_____ **3.** law of conservation of mass

**c.** This states that when two elements combine to form two or more compounds, the mass of one element that combines with a given mass of the other is in the ratio of small whole numbers.

_____ **4.** law of multiple proportions

**d.** This states that mass cannot be created or destroyed during ordinary chemical and physical changes.

**Answer the following in the space provided.**

**5.** State the five principles in Dalton's atomic theory.

**a.** _____

_____

**b.** _____

_____

**c.** _____

_____

**d.** _____

_____

**e.** _____

_____

Skills Worksheet

# Concept Review

## Section: Structure of Atoms

**In the blank at the left of each word or phrase, write the letter of the expression on the right that is most closely related.**

_____ **1.** alpha particle

_____ **2.** anode

_____ **3.** atomic number

_____ **4.** cathode

_____ **5.** Coulomb's law

_____ **6.** electron

_____ **7.** proton

_____ **8.** isotope

_____ **9.** mass number

_____ **10.** neutron

_____ **11.** nucleus

**a.** the electrode attached to the positive terminal of a voltage source

**b.** the electrode attached to the negative terminal of a voltage source

**c.** a subatomic particle that has a negative charge

**d.** an atom's central region, which is made up of protons and neutrons

**e.** a subatomic particle that has a positive charge and that composes the nucleus of an atom; the number of these particles determines the identity of an element.

**f.** the number of protons that compose the nucleus of an atom; this number is the same for all atoms of an element.

**g.** a subatomic particle that has no charge and that composes the nucleus of an atom

**h.** a small, positively charged particle, which Rutherford directed at thin, gold foil

**i.** the sum of the number of protons and neutrons of the nucleus of an atom

**j.** states that the closer two charges are, the greater the force between them; in fact, the force increases by a factor of 4 as the distance is halved.

**k.** an atom that has the same number of protons (atomic number) as other atoms of the same element but has a different number of neutrons (atomic mass)

| **Concept Review** *continued*

**Answer the following items in the space provided.**

**12.** In Thomson's cathode-ray experiment, what evidence led him to believe that the ray consisted of particles, and why did he conclude that the ray was negatively charged?

_____

_____

_____

_____

**13.** Describe the evidence for the existence of electrons.

_____

_____

_____

**14.** Describe the evidence for the existence of protons.

_____

_____

_____

**15.** Describe the evidence for the existence of neutrons.

_____

_____

_____

**16.** Describe the properties of electrons, protons, and neutrons.

_____

_____

_____

**17.** In your own words, define *isotope*.

_____

_____

_____

| Concept Review *continued*

**Use the appropriate term from the list below to fill in the blanks. Use each term only once.**

| volume | nucleus | small | alpha |
|---|---|---|---|
| positive | deflected | mass | undeflected |

18. In the Rutherford gold foil experiment, positively charged _____ particles were directed at a thin gold foil. It was found that most of the particles passed through the foil _____. However, a small number of particles were _____, some even backward. These two observations suggested that most of the _____ of an atom is empty space but that there was a central core with a charge that repelled the _____ particles. This core is a very _____ part of an atom. It contains most of the _____ of the atom and is called the _____.

19. Complete the following table.

| Isotope | Number of protons | Number of electrons | Number of neutrons | Number of particles in nucleus | Symbol for isotope |
|---|---|---|---|---|---|
| Hydrogen-2 | | | | | |
| Helium-3 | | | | | |
| Lithium-7 | | | | | |
| Beryllium-9 | | | | | |
| Boron-11 | | | | | |

20. Define *atomic number* and *mass number*.

_____

_____

_____

_____

_____

Skills Worksheet

# Concept Review

## Section: Electron Configuration

In the blanks at the left of each word or phrase, write the letter of the expression on the right that is most closely related.

_____ 1. electromagnetic spectrum

**a.** the spectrum of a few colors seen through a prism made when high-voltage current is passed through a tube of hydrogen gas at low pressure

_____ 2. electron configuration

**b.** the lowest energy state of a quantized system

_____ 3. excited state

**c.** a state in which an atom has more energy than it does at its ground state

_____ 4. ground state

**d.** a number that specifies the properties of electrons in an atom

_____ 5. Hund's rule

**e.** the arrangement of electrons in an atom

_____ 6. line-emission spectrum

**f.** a region in an atom where there is a high probability of finding electrons

_____ 7. orbital

**g.** states that two particles of a certain class cannot be in the exact same energy state

_____ 8. Pauli exclusion principle

**h.** the present-day model of the atom, in which electrons are located in orbitals

_____ 9. quantum number

**i.** states that the structure of each successive element is obtained by adding one proton to the nucleus of the atom and one electron to the lowest-energy orbital that is available

_____ 10. quantum theory

**j.** all of the frequencies or wavelengths of electromagnetic radiation

_____ 11. aufbau principle

**k.** what occurs when light strikes a metal and electrons are released

_____ 12. photoelectric effect

**l.** states that for an atom in the ground state, the number of unpaired electrons is the maximum possible and these unpaired electrons have the same spin

**Concept Review** *continued*

**Complete each statement below by writing the correct word or words in the spaces.**

**13.** All electromagnetic radiation, including visible light, can be thought of as

moving _____.

**14.** As the frequency of a wave increases, the wavelength _____.

**15.** To define the region in which electrons can be found, scientists have assigned

four _____ numbers to each electron.

**Answer the following items in the space provided.**

**16.** Using the quantum theory, how does one determine the location of an atom's electrons?

_____

_____

_____

_____

_____

_____

**17.** Compare the Rutherford, Bohr, and quantum models of an atom.

_____

_____

_____

_____

_____

_____

_____

_____

_____

**18.** Explain how the wavelengths of light emitted by an atom provide information about electron energy levels.

_____

_____

_____

_____

**19.** List the four quantum numbers, and describe their significance.

_____

_____

_____

_____

_____

_____

_____

**20.** Use the Pauli exclusion principle and the aufbau principle to write the electron configuration for the following atoms.

**a.** Chlorine

**b.** Nitrogen

**c.** Calcium

Skills Worksheet

# Concept Review

## Section: Counting Atoms

**In the blanks at the left of each word or phrase, write the letter of the expression on the right that is most closely related.**

_____ **1.** Avogadro's number

_____ **2.** atomic mass

_____ **3.** mole

_____ **4.** molar mass

**a.** the mass of an atom expressed in atomic mass units

**b.** the SI base unit used to measure the amount of a substance whose number of particles is the same as the number of atoms in 12 grams of carbon-12

**c.** the mass in grams of one mole of a substance

**d.** the number of atoms or molecules in 1 mol, equal to $6.022 \times 10^{23}$

**Answer the following items in the space provided.**

**5.** Which isotope defines the atomic mass unit, and how is the atomic mass unit defined?

_____

_____

**6.** Why is a mole used to count atoms?

_____

_____

**7.** What is the relationship between an atom's atomic mass and one mole of that atom?

_____

_____

_____

## Concept Review *continued*

**8.** The atomic mass of lithium is 6.939 amu. Would you expect the isotopes $^6_3Li$ and $^7_3Li$ to be equally common? Why or why not? If not, which isotope would you expect to be more common?

_____

_____

_____

_____

_____

**9.** What is the mass in atomic mass units of one fluorine atom?

_____

**10.** What is the mass in grams of one fluorine atom?

**11.** How many molecules are in one mole of carbon dioxide, $CO_2$?

**12.** Calculate the mass of one mole of carbon dioxide, $CO_2$.

Skills Worksheet

# Concept Review

## Section: How are Elements Organized?

**Answer the following questions in the space provided.**

1. Why do Li, Na, K, Rb, Cs, and Fr all react with Cl in a 1:1 ratio forming substances with similar properties?

   _____

   _____

   _____

2. Explain the method that John Newlands used to organize the elements.

   _____

   _____

   _____

3. What method did Dmitri Mendeleev use to arrange his periodic table?

   _____

   _____

   _____

4. Why did Mendeleev have gaps in his table? How did he use these gaps?

   _____

   _____

   _____

5. What was Henry Moseley's contribution to the periodic table?

   _____

   _____

   _____

| **Concept Review** *continued*

**6.** Why was Moseley able to resolve the discrepancies in Mendeleev's table when Mendeleev could not?

_____

_____

_____

**7.** Explain the importance of valence electrons.

_____

_____

_____

**8.** Why do elements with similar properties appear at regular intervals in the periodic table?

_____

_____

_____

**9.** How is the electron configuration similar for each element in a group?

_____

_____

_____

**10.** How is the electron configuration similar for each element in a period?

_____

_____

_____

Skills Worksheet

# Concept Review

## Section: Tour of the Periodic Table

**Complete each statement below by choosing a term from the following list. Terms may be used more than once.**

| | | | |
|---|---|---|---|
| main-group elements | halogens | metals | transition metals |
| alkaline earth metals | alkali metals | hydrogen | noble gases |

1. The _____ have a single electron in the highest occupied energy level.

2. The _____ are in the *s*- and *p*-blocks of the periodic table.

3. All the _____ have two valence electrons and get to a stable electron configuration by losing two electrons.

4. Unlike the main-group elements, each group of the _____ does not have the identical outer electron configuration.

5. The _____, the most reactive group of non-metals, achieve stable electron configurations by gaining one electron.

6. The _____ have a full set of electrons in their outermost energy level.

7. The _____ are very stable and have low reactivity.

8. The _____ are highly reactive and readily form salts with metals.

9. In general, the _____ are metals that are less reactive than the alkali metals and the alkaline earth metals.

10. The _____ are metals that lose one electron when they react with water to form alkaline solutions.

11. Most elements are _____.

12. With its one valence electron, _____ reacts with many other elements.

**Answer the following questions in the space provided.**

13. Which groups compose the main-group elements?

_____

_____

**Concept Review** *continued*

**14.** Why are the main-group elements called the *representative elements?*

_____

_____

**15.** Why are Group 2 elements less reactive than Group 1 elements?

_____

_____

**16.** Explain why a helium atmosphere is used in welding instead of an oxygen-rich atmosphere.

_____

_____

**17.** Using electron configurations, explain why the halogens readily react with the alkali metals to form salts.

_____

_____

_____

**18.** Why is an iron alloy, such as steel, preferred over pure iron?

_____

_____

_____

**Complete each statement below by writing the correct word or words in the space provided.**

**19.** The _____ include all members of Groups 1 through 12, as well as some of the elements of Groups _____ through

_____.

**20.** Elements in Groups _____ through

_____, including the two long rows below the table, are called transition elements.

**21.** In the transition elements, electrons are usually added to the

_____ orbital, which is why these elements are also

known as the _____.

## Concept Review *continued*

**22.** The _____ include all of the elements in Groups 17 and 18

as well as some members of Groups _____ through

_____ .

**23.** In the _____, electrons are being added to the 4*f* orbitals.

**24.** In the _____, electrons are being added to the 5*f* orbitals.

**25.** The _____ are unique in that all are unstable and

radioactive.

Skills Worksheet

# Concept Review

## Section: Trends in the Periodic Table

**Complete each statement below by writing the correct word or words in the space provided.**

1. The amount of energy needed to remove an electron from a specific atom is

called the _____ energy of the atom.

2. The _____ is half the distance from center to center of

two like atoms bonded together.

3. _____ is the energy change that occurs when a neutral

atom gains an electron.

4. _____ is a numerical value that reflects how much an

atom in a molecule attracts electrons.

5. As the nuclear charge increases across a period, the effective nuclear charge

_____ pulling the electrons closer to the nucleus and

_____ the size of the atom.

**Circle the letter of the choice that best answers the question.**

6. Which of the following elements has the largest atomic radius?

   **a.** boron

   **b.** aluminum

   **c.** gallium

   **d.** indium

7. Which of the following elements has the smallest ionization energy?

   **a.** potassium

   **b.** arsenic

   **c.** nitrogen

   **d.** bismuth

**8.** Which of the following elements has the largest electronegativity?

   **a.** lithium

   **b.** carbon

   **c.** chlorine

   **d.** iodine

## Answer the following questions in the space provided.

**9.** Explain why the exact size of an atom is difficult to determine.

_____

_____

_____

**10.** Which metal has the larger radius, Li or Na? Why?

_____

_____

**11.** What is electron shielding?

_____

_____

_____

**12.** Explain the large decrease in atomic radii as you move across a period from Group 1 to Group 14.

_____

_____

_____

**13.** Explain why ionization energies tend to decrease down a group.

_____

_____

_____

**Concept Review** *continued*

**14.** Explain the large increase in electronegativity as you move across a period.

_____

_____

_____

_____

**15.** Complete the following table.

| | General Trends | |
|---|---|---|
| | **From left to right across a period** | **Down a group** |
| **Ionization energy** | | |
| **Atomic radius** | | |
| **Electronegativity** | | |
| **Ionic size** | | |
| **Electron affinity** | | |

Skills Worksheet

# Concept Review

## Section: Where Did the Elements Come From?

**Complete each statement below by writing the correct terms or terms.**

1. Most of the atoms in living things come from just six elements,

   _____, _____,

   _____, _____,

   _____, and _____.

2. Immediately after the big bang, temperatures were extremely high and only

   _____ could exist.

3. As the universe began to cool, energy was converted to

   _____, in the form of _____,

   _____, and _____.

4. As the universe continued to cool, these particles joined and formed the first

   two elements, _____ and _____.

5. The temperatures in stars get high enough to fuse _____

   nuclei with one another, forming elements of still higher atomic numbers.

6. Massive atoms such as iron and nickel form by repeated

   _____.

7. When a massive star has converted almost all its core hydrogen and helium

   into heavier elements, it collapses and blows apart in an explosion called a

   _____ forming elements heavier than iron.

8. The nuclear reaction that changes one nucleus into another by radioactive

   disintegration or by bombardment with other particles is called

   _____.

| Concept Review *continued*

**9.** Elements that chemists have created are called _____

elements.

**10.** The special equipment that scientists use to create elements are called

_____ .

**Answer the following questions in the space provided.**

**11.** There are 93 naturally occurring elements, yet the periodic table contains 113 elements. Briefly explain the difference in the two numbers.

_____

_____

_____

**12.** Why are there limits to the synthetic elements that a cyclotron can produce?

_____

_____

_____

**13.** How does a synchrotron accelerate particles to create synthetic elements?

_____

_____

_____

**14.** What is the difficulty in identifying superheavy elements?

_____

_____

_____

Skills Worksheet

# Concept Review

## Section: Simple Ions

**Complete each statement below by choosing a term from the following list. Terms may be used more than once.**

| | | | |
|---|---|---|---|
| 10 | 11 | ion | octet |
| 12 | 13 | anion | cation |

**1.** An atom or group of atoms that has a positive or negative electric charge

because it has lost or gained electrons is a(n) _____.

**2.** The sodium ion has _____ protons, _____ neutrons,

and _____ electrons.

**3.** In most chemical reactions, atoms tend to match the outer electron configura-

tion of the noble gases. This is called the _____ rule.

**Complete each statement below by writing the correct term or phrase.**

**4.** An anion is an ion with a _____ charge.

**5.** _____ electrons occupy the outermost energy level of an atom.

**6.** The chloride ion and the chlorine atom have _____ electron

configurations.

**7.** A cation is an ion with a _____ charge.

**8.** Many stable ions have an electron configuration of a _____.

**Answer the following questions in the space provided.**

**9.** How do the outer-shell electron configurations for ions of Group 1, Group 2,
and Group 15, Group 16, and Group 17 elements compare with those of the
noble gases?

_____

_____

_____

_____

**Concept Review** *continued*

**10.** What do you notice about all of the ionic charges for Group 1? Group 2? Group 15? Group 16? Group 17?

_____

_____

_____

**11.** How many valance electrons do atoms in Group 1, Group 2, Group 15, Group 16, and Group 17 have?

_____

_____

**12.** State the octet rule.

_____

_____

_____

**13.** Ions of calcium, fluorine, magnesium, and iodine have electron configurations that are similar to which noble gases?

_____

_____

**14.** Explain why the properties of ions differ from those of their parent atoms.

_____

_____

_____

**15.** Why do atoms of metals form cations?

_____

_____

_____

**16.** Why do atoms of nonmetals form anions?

_____

_____

_____

Skills Worksheet
# Concept Review

## Section: Ionic Bonding and Salts
**Complete each statement below by writing the correct term or phrase.**

1. The arrangement of ion in sodium chloride shows that each ion is surrounded by _____ oppositely-charged ions.

2. The attractive force between sodium ions and chloride ions results in an arrangement of ions in repeating units arranged to form a _____.

3. In the sodium chloride crystal arrangement, the net effect is that the _____ between oppositely charged ions is significantly greater than _____ between ions of like charge.

4. The arrangement of cations and anions depends on the _____ and the _____ of the ions.

**Complete each statement below by choosing a term from the following list.**

lattice energy          salt          unit cell          crystal lattice

5. The specific way in which atoms are arranged in an ionic compound is called the _____.

6. The _____ is the simplest repeating unit of a crystal structure.

7. A _____ is a compound that results when an ionic bond is formed between a cation and an anion.

8. When 1 mole of a salt is formed from gaseous ions, _____ is released.

**Answer the following questions in the space provided.**

9. Briefly describe why the structure of ionic compounds causes the compounds to be hard.

_____

_____

_____

**| Concept Review** *continued*

10. When a force is applied to an ionic compound and the ions are repositioned so that like-charged ions are located next to each other, what happens to the compound?

_____

_____

_____

11. How is an ionic bond formed?

_____

_____

_____

12. Define *salt*.

_____

_____

_____

13. Why do ionic compounds have high melting points and high boiling points?

_____

_____

_____

_____

_____

14. Why are ionic solids generally poor conductors of electricity?

_____

_____

15. When are salts excellent conductors of electricity?

_____

_____

_____

**16.** Name five characteristics of ionic compounds.

_____

_____

_____

_____

_____

_____

**17.** How do these five properties relate to the nature of ionic bonds?

_____

_____

_____

_____

_____

_____

**18.** Describe the structure of salt crystals.

_____

_____

_____

_____

_____

Skills Worksheet

# Concept Review

## Section: Names and Formulas of Ionic Compounds

**Complete each statement below by choosing a term from the following list. Terms may be used more than once.**

| | | | |
|---|---|---|---|
| cations | electroneutrality | *-ide* | Roman numerals |
| polyatomic | ionic | subscript | |

1. Having equal amounts of positive and negative charges is called

   _____.

2. An electrically charged group of two or more bonded atoms that functions as

   a single ion is a _____ ion.

3. Collections of _____ are never found without a similar number of anions (or sometimes electrons) nearby to effectively neutralize the charges.

4. The names for _____ come from the element from which they are formed.

5. When an element forms two or more positive ions, the ions are distinguished

   by using _____ to indicate the charge.

6. The name of a simple anion is formed by changing the ending of the element

   name to _____.

7. A _____ is a whole number written below and to the right of an element's symbol, and it is used to denote the number of atoms in a formula.

8. Any chemical compound that is composed of oppositely charged ions is called

   a(n) _____ compound.

### Write the formula for the following compounds.

9. potassium bromide

   _____

10. barium fluoride

    _____

11. tin(IV) oxide

    _____

**12.** cesium bromide

_____

**13.** cobalt(II) bromide

_____

**14.** mercury(I) sulfide

_____

**15.** aluminum iodide

_____

**Write the names of the following, and include Roman numerals if needed.**

**16.** $Cu^+$ _____

**17.** $Cl^-$ _____

**18.** $O^{2-}$ _____

**19.** $P^{3-}$ _____

**20.** $Na^+$ _____

**21.** $Mg^{2+}$ _____

**22.** NaCl _____

**23.** ZnS _____

**24.** $Fe_2O_3$ _____

**25.** $Mg_3N_2$ _____

**26.** ZnO _____

**27.** NaI _____

**28.** $Cu_2O$ _____

**29.** $CaCl_2$ _____

**30.** $CrCl_3$ _____

**31.** HgO _____

**Answer the following questions in the space provided.**

**32.** How are polyatomic salts named?

_____

_____

_____

**33.** How do the formulas for atomic salts relate to their names?

_____

_____

**Choose the statement from Column B that best matches the term in Column A, and write the corresponding letter in the space provided.**

**Column A**

_____**34.** *-ite* and *-ate*

_____**35.** monohydrogen

_____**36.** dihydrogen

_____**37.** *thio-*

**Column B**

**a.** indicates the presence of one hydrogen atom in the ion

**b.** the endings of polyatomic ions containing oxygen

**c.** "replace an oxygen by a sulfur" in the anion

**d.** indicates the presence of two hydrogens in the ion

**Write the name for the following compounds that contain polyatomic ions.**

**38.** $K_2Cr_2O_7$ _____

**39.** $KClO_2$ _____

**40.** $Fe(ClO_3)_3$ _____

**41.** $Na_2SO_4$ _____

**42.** $Na_2SO_3$ _____

**43.** $KMnO_4$ _____

**44.** $Pb(NO_3)_2$ _____

**Write the formula for the following compounds containing polyatomic ions.**

**45.** lead (IV) chromate _____

**46.** sodium hypochlorite _____

**47.** magnesium nitrate _____

**48.** sodium peroxide _____

**49.** hydrogen cyanide _____

**50.** aluminum hydroxide _____

**51.** ammonium sulfate _____

Skills Worksheet

# Concept Review

## Section: Covalent Bonds

**Answer the following items in the space provided.**

**1.** How does a covalent bond form between two atoms?

_____

_____

_____

_____

**2.** Why is the $H_2$ molecule more stable than two separate hydrogen atoms?

_____

_____

_____

**3.** Explain why the stability described in item 2 does or does not hold true for most covalent bonds.

_____

_____

_____

_____

_____

**4.** How does a covalent bond differ from an ionic bond?

_____

_____

_____

_____

**Concept Review** *continued*

**5.** What is a molecular orbital?

_____

_____

_____

_____

_____

**6.** Describe the potential energy change that occurs when two hydrogen atoms approach each other and form a covalent bond.

_____

_____

_____

_____

_____

**7.** In terms of energy, why is the H-H bond stable?

_____

_____

_____

_____

_____

_____

**8.** Why is bond length an average rather than a fixed number?

_____

_____

_____

_____

_____

_____

**Concept Review** *continued*

**9.** Describe the typical physical properties of substances that have metallic, ionic, and covalent bonds.

_____

_____

_____

_____

_____

_____

_____

_____

_____

_____

**Complete each statement below by choosing a term from the following list. Terms may be used more than once.**

| energy | electronegativity | dipole | polar covalent |
| nonpolar covalent | length | ionic | |

**10.** Bond _____ is defined as the average distance between two bonded atoms at their minimum potential energy.

**11.** Bond _____ is defined as the energy required to break the chemical bond between two atoms and separate them.

**12.** The tendency of an atom to attract bonding electrons to itself when it bonds

with another atom is called its _____.

**13.** A _____ bond is an attraction between two atoms in which bonding electrons are shared equally between the atoms.

**14.** A _____ bond is an attraction between two atoms in which bonding electrons are localized on the more electronegative atom.

| Concept Review *continued*

**15.** A _____ molecule is one that has a partial positive charge at one end and a partial negative charge at the opposite end.

**16.** In general, if the difference in electronegativity between two atoms is between 0 and 0.5, the bond formed is _____.

**17.** If the electronegativity difference between two atoms is between 0.5 and 2.1, the bond formed is _____.

**18.** If the electronegativity difference between two atoms is greater than 2.1, the bond formed is _____.

**Answer the following items in the space provided.**

**19.** Predict the type of bond that is present between sodium and fluorine in sodium fluoride, NaF, which is used in fluoridation of drinking water.

_____

**20.** Predict the type of bond present between carbon and hydrogen in polyethylene.

_____

**21.** Predict the type of bond present between carbon and sulfur in vulcanized rubber.

_____

**22.** Predict the type of bond present between carbon and fluorine in the polymer Teflon.

_____

**23.** Predict the type of bond that is present between phosphorus and oxygen in a DNA molecule.

_____

Skills Worksheet

# Concept Review

## Section: Drawing and Naming Molecules

**Complete each statement below by choosing a term from the following list. Terms may be used more than once.**

triple    double    single    resonance    Lewis    valence    unshared

1. An electron in the outermost energy level of an atom that can participate in

   bonding is called a(n) _____ electron.

2. A structure in which atomic symbols represent nuclei and inner-shell
   electrons and in which dots are used to represent valence electrons is called

   a(n) _____ structure.

3. A possible Lewis structure of a molecule for which more than one Lewis

   structure can be written is called a(n) _____ structure.

4. A covalent bond in which two atoms share two pairs of electrons is called

   a(n) _____ bond.

5. A covalent bond in which two atoms share three pairs of electrons is called

   a(n) _____ bond.

6. A bond in which two atoms share one pair of electrons is a _____
   bond.

7. A nonbonding pair of electrons in the valence shell of an atom is called a(n)

   _____ pair.

**Answer the following items in the space provided.**

8. Methanol, $CH_3OH$, can be used as a solvent, as an antifreeze, and in the
   production of formaldehyde. Draw the Lewis structure for methanol.

9. Propane, $C_3H_8$, is a common fuel for gas barbecue grills. Draw the Lewis
   structure for propane.

| Concept Review *continued*

**10.** Draw the Lewis structure for water, $H_2O$.

**11.** Draw the Lewis structure for carbon monoxide, CO.

**12.** Draw the Lewis structure for the rocket propellant nitryl fluoride, $NO_2F$.

**13.** Draw the Lewis structures for $SO_3^{2-}$.

**Answer the following item in the space provided.**

**14.** Explain the difference between single, double, and triple bonds.

_____

_____

_____

_____

_____

**Concept Review** *continued*

**Use the system of prefixes and the rule for suffixes to name the following compounds.**

**15.** $PbCl_2$

_____

**16.** $KCl$

_____

**17.** $LiO_2$

_____

**18.** $As_2O_3$

_____

**19.** $PBr_3$

_____

**20.** $SF_4$

_____

**21.** $N_2O_5$

_____

**Write the formulas for the following compounds.**

**22.** nitrogen monoxide

_____

**23.** carbon dioxide

_____

**24.** carbon tetrachloride

_____

**25.** carbon disulfide

_____

Skills Worksheet

# Concept Review

## Section: Molecular Shapes

**Answer the following items in the space provided.**

1. What does VSEPR theory predict?

   _____

   _____

2. Draw the Lewis structure for each of the following molecules, and use the VSEPR theory to predict the shape of each.

   **a.** $CH_4$

   **b.** $CCl_4$

   **c.** $NO_2$

3. How does one unbonded pair of electrons affect the shape of a molecule?

   _____

   _____

   _____

   _____

**Concept Review** *continued*

**4.** How do multiple unbonded pairs of electrons affect the shape of a molecule?

_____

_____

_____

_____

**5.** What evidence is there to support the idea that opposite polar ends of molecules attract each other?

_____

_____

_____

_____

**6.** How do polarity and shape of molecules relate to the properties of a substance?

_____

_____

_____

_____

_____

_____

_____

Skills Worksheet

# Concept Review

## Section: Avogadro's Number and Molar Conversions

**Solve the following problems, and write your answer in the space provided.**

  1. Determine the number of atoms present in 4.00 mol of aluminum.

  2. Determine the number of atoms present in 1.55 mol of sodium.

  3. Convert $2.65 \times 10^{25}$ atoms of fluorine to moles of fluorine atoms.

  4. Convert $4.26 \times 10^{25}$ molecules of hydrogen, $H_2$, to moles of hydrogen, $H_2$.

  5. Convert $1.75 \times 10^{26}$ atoms of potassium to moles of potassium.

**6.** Determine the mass in grams of 7.20 mol of antimony.

**7.** Determine the mass in grams of 0.500 mol of uranium.

**8.** Determine the mass in grams of 0.750 mol of francium.

**9.** A sample of lead has a mass of 150.0 g. What amount of lead in moles does the sample contain?

**10.** A sample of gold has a mass of $5.00 \times 10^{-3}$ g. What amount of gold in moles does the sample contain?

Skills Worksheet )

# Concept Review

## Section: Relative Atomic Mass and Chemical Formulas

**Solve the following problems, and write your answer in the space provided.**

**1.** Calculate the average atomic mass of rubidium if 72.17% of its atoms have a mass of 84.91 amu and 27.83% of its atoms have a mass of 86.91 amu.

**2.** Calculate the average atomic mass of chlorine if 75.77% of its atoms have a mass of 34.97 amu and 24.23% of its atoms have a mass of 36.96 amu.

**3.** Calculate the molar mass of calcium phosphate, $Ca_3(PO_4)_2$.

**4.** Calculate the molar mass of rutile, $TiO_2$, a mineral used in coloring glass.

**Concept Review** *continued*

**5.** Calculate the molar mass of baking soda, sodium hydrogen carbonate, $NaHCO_3$.

**6.** Calculate the molar mass of phenol, $C_6H_5OH$.

**7.** Calculate the molar mass of acetylene, $C_2H_2$, a gas used in welding.

**8.** Calculate the molar mass of water, $H_2O$.

Name _____  Class _____  Date _____

# Concept Review

## Section: Formulas and Percentage Composition

**Solve the following problems, and write your answer in the space provided.**

1. The mineral greenockite is a yellow sulfide of cadmium that is 78.0% cadmium and 22.0% sulfur. Determine the empirical formula of greenockite.

2. What is the empirical formula for a compound of aluminum and fluorine that is 32% aluminum and 68% fluorine?

3. What is the empirical formula for a compound that is 26.56% potassium, 35.41% chromium, and 38.03% oxygen?

4. What is the empirical formula for a compound that is 33.36% calcium, 26.69% sulfur, and 40.00% oxygen?

**5.** What is the empirical formula for a compound that is 29.44% calcium, 23.55% sulfur, and 47.01% oxygen? This compound is a common ingredient in plaster.

**6.** The empirical formula of a compound is CH. The experimental molar mass is 78.12 g/mol. Determine the molecular formula of the compound.

**7.** The empirical formula of a compound is $CH_2O$. The experimental molar mass is 60.06 g/mol. Determine the molecular formula of the compound.

**8.** The empirical formula of a substance is $P_2O_5$. The experimental molar mass is 283.89 g/mol. Determine the molecular formula of the compound.

**Concept Review** *continued*

**9.** The empirical formula of a substance is $BH_3$. The experimental molar mass is 27.67 g/mol. Determine the molecular formula of the compound.

**10.** The empirical formula of a compound is CH. The experimental molar mass is 26.04 g/mol. Determine the molecular formula of the compound.

**11.** Quartz has the chemical formula $SiO_2$. What is the percentage composition of this compound?

**12.** Urea, a component in fertilizer, has the chemical formula, $CO(NH_2)_2$. What is the percentage composition of this compound?

**Concept Review** *continued*

**13.** Fructose, a sweetener in soft drinks, has the chemical formula $C_6H_{12}O_6$. What is the percentage composition of this compound?

**14.** Which of two common ingredients in garden fertilizers, ammonium sulfate, $(NH_4)_2SO_4$, or ammonium phosphate, $(NH_4)_3PO_4$, has a greater percentage of nitrogen?

**15.** Which compound has the greater percentage of zinc—smithsonite, $ZnCO_3$, or sphalerite, $ZnS$?

Skills Worksheet

# Concept Review

## Section: Describing Chemical Reactions

**Answer the following items in the space provided.**

1. What is a chemical reaction?

   _____

   _____

   _____

2. Give three examples of a chemical change that has occurred in your home.

   a. _____

   b. _____

   c. _____

3. State nine observations that suggest that a chemical reaction has occurred.

   a. _____

   b. _____

   c. _____

   d. _____

   e. _____

   f. _____

   g. _____

   h. _____

   i. _____

4. What laboratory evidence do you need to show that a chemical reaction has taken place?

   _____

   _____

   _____

**5.** List five processes that are physical changes.

   **a.** _____

   **b.** _____

   **c.** _____

   **d.** _____

   **e.** _____

**6.** Identify the following events as examples of either physical or chemical changes. For those that describe chemical changes, identify the reactants and the products.

   **a.** Silver nitrate solution is added to another solution, producing a white solid.

_____

_____

   **b.** Gasoline gives off fumes.

_____

_____

   **c.** Sea water evaporates, leaving salt deposits.

_____

_____

   **d.** A marshmallow is burned over a campfire.

_____

_____

**7.** If you slide a safety match across an untreated striking surface, will it light? Explain.

_____

_____

_____

**8.** Compare a word equation and a formula equation.

_____

_____

_____

_____

| Concept Review *continued*

**Answer the following items in the space provided.**

9. In a chemical reaction that releases energy, energy is a _____ of the reaction.

10. In a chemical reaction that absorbs energy, energy is a _____ of the reaction.

11. Supply the missing information in the table below.

| Symbol | Meaning |
|---|---|
| $\rightarrow$ | |
| $\rightleftarrows$ | |
| | reactants are heated; temperature is not specified |
| $(s), (l), (g)$ | |
| | chemical formula of a catalyst; a substance added to speed up a reaction |
| $(aq)$ | |

Skills Worksheet

# Concept Review

## Section: Balancing Chemical Equations

**Answer the following items in the space provided.**

**1.** State the law of conservation of mass.

_____

_____

_____

**2.** Using the law of conservation of mass, explain why the following reaction is wrong: $HCl + NaOH \rightarrow NaCl$.

_____

_____

_____

**3.** How can you tell when an equation is balanced?

_____

_____

**4.** Consider the following balanced equation for the reaction between iron metal and water:

$$3Fe + 4H_2O \rightarrow Fe_3O_4 + 4H_2$$

**a.** Is the 3 in 3Fe a subscript or a coefficient?

_____

**b.** What is the subscript in the water molecule?

_____

**c.** How does changing a coefficient differ from changing a subscript?

_____

_____

**d.** Why is Fe balanced as 3Fe instead of $Fe_3$?

_____

_____

_____

   **e.** What do the 4 and 2 signify in $4H_2$? How many hydrogen atoms are there?

   _____

   _____

   _____

**5.** Water vapor and nitrogen dioxide gas, $NO_2$, are combined to manufacture
   ammonia. A byproduct of this reaction is oxygen gas. Write the balanced
   chemical equation for this reaction.

   _____

**6.** Iron can be obtained by reacting the naturally occurring ore hematite, $Fe_2O_3$,
   with carbon. The carbon is converted to $CO_2$. Write the balanced chemical
   equation for this reaction.

   _____

**7.** Granules of zinc oxide, ZnO, will react with hydrochloric acid, HCl, to form
   zinc chloride, $ZnCl_2$, and water. Write the balanced chemical equation for this
   reaction.

   _____

**8.** A reaction between copper and nitric acid, $HNO_3$, produces copper(II) nitrate,
   $Cu(NO_3)_2$, nitrogen monoxide, NO, and water. Write the balanced chemical
   equation for this reaction.

   _____

**9.** Ethane, $C_2H_6$, reacts with molecular oxygen to produce carbon dioxide and
   water. Write the balanced chemical equation for this reaction.

   _____

Skills Worksheet

# Concept Review

## Section: Classifying Chemical Reactions

**Answer the following items in the space provided.**

1. Your reactants are two elements. Your product is a binary compound. What type of reaction do you have?

   _____

2. Your reactants are a hydrocarbon and oxygen. Your products are carbon dioxide and water. What type of reaction do you have?

   _____

3. You have one reactant and two elements for products. What type of reaction do you have?

   _____

4. Your reactants are an element and a compound that is not a hydrocarbon. What type of reaction do you probably have?

   _____

5. Your reactants are two compounds composed of ions. What type of reaction do you probably have?

   _____

**Classify the reaction type for each of the following reactions. Briefly explain the reason for your selection.**

6. $2C_6H_{14}(l) + 19O_2(g) \rightarrow 14H_2O(g) + 12CO_2(g)$

   _____

   _____

7. $4Fe(s) + 3O_2(g) \rightarrow 2Fe_2O_3(s)$

   _____

   _____

8. $2AlCl_3(s) \rightarrow 2Al(s) + 3Cl_2(g)$

   _____

   _____

**9.** Write a balanced chemical equation for the combustion of $C_2H_2$ gas. One of the products is carbon dioxide. Be sure to include states of matter.

_____

**Determine whether each of the following reactions can occur. If the reaction does occur, write the complete, balanced equation. If the reaction does not occur, explain why not.**

**10.** $2Cr(s) + SnCl_4(aq) \rightarrow$

_____

_____

_____

**11.** $2Ni(s) + MgSO_4(aq) \rightarrow$

_____

_____

_____

**12.** $Zn(s) + CdCl_2(aq) \rightarrow$

_____

_____

_____

**13.** $Ag(s) + ZnCO_3(aq) \rightarrow$

_____

_____

_____

**14.** Write a balanced chemical equation for the reaction of hydrochloric acid and magnesium metal. One of the products is magnesium chloride, $MgCl_2$. Be sure to include states of matter. What kind of reaction is this?

_____

_____

Skills Worksheet

# Concept Review

## Section: Writing Net Ionic Equations

**Answer the following items in the space provided.**

1. What are spectator ions?

_____

_____

_____

2. Write a total ionic equation for each of the following reactions.

   **a.** copper(II) sulfate + iron → iron(III) + copper

   _____

   **b.** potassium iodide + chlorine → potassium chloride + iodine

   _____

   **c.** $Mg(s) + CuSO_4(aq) \rightarrow MgSO_4(aq) + Cu(s)$

   _____

   **d.** $2Au(NO_3)_3(aq) + 3Zn(s) \rightarrow 2Au(s) + 3Zn(NO_3)_2(aq)$

   _____

   **e.** $NiBr_2(aq) + Co(s) \rightarrow Ni(s) + CoBr_2(aq)$

   _____

   **f.** $BaCl_2(aq) + CuSO_4(aq) \rightarrow BaSO_4(s) + CuCl_2(aq)$

   _____

3. Identify the spectator ions in each of the reactions in item 2.

   **a.** _____

   **b.** _____

   **c.** _____

   **d.** _____

   **e.** _____

   **f.** _____

**Concept Review** *continued*

**4.** Write the net ionic equation for each reaction in item 2.

a. _____

b. _____

c. _____

d. _____

e. _____

f. _____

**5.** Write a balanced chemical equation for the double-displacement reaction of barium chloride solution, $BaCl_2$, and sodium carbonate solution, $Na_2CO_3$. What is the net ionic equation?

_____

_____

_____

Skills Worksheet

# Concept Review

## Section: Calculating Quantities in Reactions

**Complete each statement below by writing the correct term or phrase.**

**1.** All stoichiometric calculations involving equations use _____ ratios.

**2.** When solving stoichiometric problems, you must _____ the equation first.

**3.** Balanced equations give the _____ numbers of moles of substances.

**4.** _____ in chemical equations provide mole ratios that can be used as conversion factors.

**5.** The conversion factor for converting between mass and moles is the _____ of the substance.

**6.** In making calculations involving _____, you must convert volume to mass.

**7.** To convert from volume to mass, you can use the _____ of the substance as the conversion factor.

**8.** When calculating the number of particles, you can use _____ as the conversion factor.

**In the blanks at the left, write the letter of the choice that best completes the statement or answers the question. Consider the following problem when answering:**

**What mass of sulfuric acid is required to neutralize 2.65 g of potassium hydroxide? The products of the reaction are potassium sulfate and water.**

_____ **9.** What should you do first after reading the problem carefully?
    **a.** Estimate the answer.
    **b.** Calculate the molar mass of sulfuric acid.
    **c.** Write a balanced chemical equation.
    **d.** Convert all masses to moles.

_____ **10.** What should you do before setting up the problem?
    **a.** Determine the densities.
    **b.** Calculate molar masses.
    **c.** Convert all masses to moles.
    **d.** Estimate the answer.

_____11. How should you check your setup?
    **a.** by recalculating molar masses
    **b.** by checking to see if the result will have the correct units
    **c.** by estimating the answer
    **d.** by writing a balanced chemical equation

_____12. What should you round off?
    **a.** the result of each step
    **b.** all data values
    **c.** only the final answer
    **d.** nothing

_____13. Which of the following is *least* likely to help you verify the final result?
    **a.** estimating the answer by using rounded numbers
    **b.** determining whether the answer is reasonable for the conditions of the problem
    **c.** rechecking all molar masses
    **d.** writing a balanced chemical equation

**Answer the following items in the space provided.**

**14.** Determine the number of grams of phosphorus formed for each 1.00 g of $Ca_3(PO_4)_2$ used in the production of phosphorus in an electric furnace.

$$Ca_3(PO_4)_2(s) + 3SiO_2(s) + 5C(s) \rightarrow 3CaSiO_3(s) + 5CO(g) + 2P(s)$$

**15.** How many grams of aluminum chloride are produced when 18 g of aluminum are reacted with an excess of hydrochloric acid?

$$2Al(s) + 6HCl(aq) \rightarrow 2AlCl_3(aq) + 3H_2(g)$$

| Concept Review *continued*

**16.** How many grams of ethanol, $C_2H_5OH$, can be made by the fermentation of 1150 g of glucose, $C_6H_{12}O_6$?

$$C_6H_{12}O_6(l) \rightarrow 2C_2H_5OH(l) + 2CO_2(g)$$

**17.** How many moles of oxygen are required for the combustion of 25.5 g of magnesium?

$$2Mg(s) + O_2(g) \rightarrow 2MgO(s)$$

**18.** How many grams of $CO_2$ are produced from the burning of 1.0 mol of amyl alcohol?

$$2C_5H_{11}OH(l) + 15O_2(g) \rightarrow 10CO_2(g) + 12H_2O(g)$$

**19.** How many moles of nitromethane are needed to form 500.0 g of chloropicrin, $CCl_3NO_2$, a chemical used in the production of insecticides?

$$CH_3NO_2(l) + 3Cl_2(g) \rightarrow CCl_3NO_2(l) + 3HCl(g)$$

**Concept Review** *continued*

**20.** How many liters of oxygen are produced from the decomposition of 122 g of potassium chlorate? The density of oxygen is 1.33 g/L.

$$2KClO_3(s) \rightarrow 2KCl(s) + 3O_2(g)$$

**21.** How many grams of potassium chloride are formed by the decomposition of sufficient potassium chlorate to yield 3.4 L of oxygen? Remember that the density of oxygen is 1.33 g/L.

$$2KClO_3(s) \rightarrow 2KCl(s) + 3O_2(g)$$

**22.** How many liters of phosphine gas are produced when 910 g of calcium phosphide react with water? The density of phosphine gas is 1.517 g/L.

$$Ca_3P_2(s) + 6H_2O(l) \rightarrow 3Ca(OH)_2(s) + 2PH_3(g)$$

**23.** How many grams of air are required to complete the combustion of 93 g of phosphorus to diphosphorus pentoxide, assuming the air to be 23% oxygen by mass?

$$4P(s) + 5O_2(g) \rightarrow 2P_2O_5(s)$$

## Concept Review *continued*

**24.** How many metric tons of carbon dioxide can be produced from the combustion of 5.00 metric tons of coke that is 85.5% carbon?

$$C(s) + O_2(g) \rightarrow CO_2(g)$$

**25.** If 100. mL of carbon disulfide (density = 1.26 g/mL) is burned completely, how many liters of $SO_2$ and of $CO_2$ are formed?

$$CS_2(l) + 3O_2(g) \rightarrow CO_2(g) + 2SO_2(g)$$

Skills Worksheet

# Concept Review

## Section: Limiting Reactants and Percentage Yield

**Complete each statement below by choosing a term from the following list. Terms may be used more than once.**

excess        product        limiting        stoichiometric

percentage    actual         theoretical

**1.** A(n) _____ reactant is not completely used up in a chemical reaction.

**2.** A(n) _____ reactant is used up first and thus controls the

quantity of _____ that can be formed in a chemical reaction.

**3.** The reactant that runs out first is the _____ reactant.

**4.** The limiting reactant should be used in _____ calculations to determine the maximum amount of product expected.

**5.** Cost is a factor in selecting the _____ reactant.

**6.** In industry, the least expensive reactant is usually used as the

_____ reactant. In this way, the more expensive reactant is completely used up, while some of the cheaper reactant is left over.

**7.** The _____ yield is a way to describe reaction efficiency.

**8.** The percentage yield describes how close the _____ yield

is to the _____ yield.

**9.** The _____ yield must be measured experimentally.

**10.** The percentage yield figures can be used to predict what the

_____ yield will likely be.

**Answer the following items in the space provided.**

**11.** When 3.00 g of Mg is ignited in 2.20 g of pure oxygen, what is the limiting reactant? What is the theoretical yield of MgO?

$$2Mg(s) + O_2(g) \rightarrow 2MgO(s)$$

**12.** When 32 g of $O_2$ reacts with 23 g of $C_2H_5OH$, what is the limiting reactant? What is the theoretical yield in grams of $CO_2$?

$$C_2H_5OH(l) + 3O_2(g) \rightarrow 2CO_2(g) + 3H_2O(l)$$

**13.** What is the limiting reactant when 154 g of Ag reacts with 189 g of $HNO_3$? What is the theoretical yield in grams of $AgNO_3$?

$$3Ag(s) + 4HNO_3(aq) \rightarrow 3AgNO_3(aq) + NO(g) + 2H_2O(l)$$

**14.** A student used 1.34 g of silver to produce silver nitrate. The actual yield was 2.01 g. Calculate the percentage yield.

$$3Ag(s) + 4HNO_3(aq) \rightarrow 3AgNO_3(aq) + NO(g) + 2H_2O(l)$$

**15.** To prepare the paint pigment chrome yellow, $PbCrO_4$, a student started with 5.552 g of $Pb(NO_3)_2$. The actual yield of $PbCrO_4$ was 5.096 g. Calculate the theoretical yield and the percentage yield.

$$Pb(NO_3)_2(aq) + Na_2CrO_4(aq) \rightarrow PbCrO_4(s) + 2NaNO_3(aq)$$

**16.** Determine the actual yield in grams of MgO when 20.0 g of magnesium is burned in air. The percentage yield of the reaction is 97.9%.

$$2Mg(s) + O_2(g) \rightarrow 2MgO(s)$$

**17.** Determine the actual yield of $Fe_2O_3$ when 10.0 g of iron(II) sulfide is burned in air. The percentage yield of the reaction is 88.1%.

$$4FeS(s) + 7O_2(g) \rightarrow 2Fe_2O_3(s) + 4SO_2(g)$$

**18.** Determine the actual yield in grams of $CCl_4$ if 175.0 g of $Cl_2$ reacts with methane. The percentage yield of the reaction is 75.4%.

$$CH_4(g) + 4Cl_2(g) \rightarrow CCl_4(g) + 4HCl(g)$$

Name _____ Class _____ Date _____

Skills Worksheet

# Concept Review

## Section: Stoichiometry and Cars

**In the blanks at left, write the letter of the choice that best answers the question.**

_____ **1.** How many moles of $N_2$ gas are generated from 0.50 mol of $NaN_3$ used in an air bag? The reaction equation is $2NaN_3(s) \rightarrow 2Na(s) + 3N_2(g)$.
  **a.** 3.0
  **b.** 1.5
  **c.** 0.75
  **d.** 2.0

_____ **2.** How many moles of isooctane will produce 6.0 mol of $H_2O$? The reaction equation is $2C_8H_{18}(g) + 25O_2(g) \rightarrow 16CO_2(g) + 18H_2O(g)$.
  **a.** 3.0
  **b.** 0.67
  **c.** 9.0
  **d.** 2.0

_____ **3.** How many moles of carbon dioxide are produced when 5.0 mol of $O_2$ is used in the reaction $2C_8H_{18}(g) + 25O_2(g) \rightarrow 16CO_2(g) + 18H_2O(g)$?
  **a.** 80
  **b.** 0.40
  **c.** 1.6
  **d.** 3.2

_____ **4.** How many moles of sodium oxide are produced if 0.5 mol of Fe is produced in the reaction $6Na(s) + Fe_2O_3(s) \rightarrow 3Na_2O(s) + 2Fe(s)$?
  **a.** 6.0
  **b.** 0.75
  **c.** 1.5
  **d.** 12

_____ **5.** Why do designers of air bags use stoichiometry?
  **a.** to ensure that air bags inflate correctly
  **b.** to ensure that air bags do not overinflate
  **c.** to ensure that air bags inflate quickly enough
  **d.** All of the above

Name _____ Class _____ Date _____

**Answer the following items in the space provided.**

**6.** Use the concept of limiting reactants to explain why fuel-air ratios affect the performance of an engine.

_____

_____

_____

**7.** What mass of sodium azide must be included in an air bag to generate 68.0 L of $N_2$? Use 0.916 g/L as the density of nitrogen gas.

$$2NaN_3(s) \rightarrow 2Na(s) + 3N_2(g)$$

**8.** How many grams of air must react with 375 mL of isooctane for complete combustion to occur? Assume the air to be 23% oxygen by mass. The density of oxygen is 1.33 g/L, and the density of isooctane is 0.692 g/mL.

$$2C_8H_{18}(l) + 25O_2(g) \rightarrow 16CO_2(g) + 18H_2O(g)$$

**9.** Nitrogen dioxide from exhaust reacts with oxygen to form ozone. How many grams of ozone, $O_3$, could be produced from 4.30 g of $NO_2$?

$$NO_2(g) + O_2(g) \rightarrow NO(g) + O_3(g)$$

Skills Worksheet

# Concept Review

## Section: Energy Transfer

**Complete each statement below by choosing a term from the following list. Use each term only once.**

| | | | |
|---|---|---|---|
| intensive | enthalpy | heat | higher |
| extensive | temperature | physical | lower |

1. Temperature and heat are different but related _____ properties.

2. If a sample has a(n) _____ temperature than its surroundings, energy is transferred from the sample. If the temperature of the sample is _____ than its surroundings, energy is transferred to the sample. The energy transferred between objects that are at different temperatures is _____. The _____ of a sample is a measure of the average kinetic energy of the particles in a sample.

3. The temperature of a sample does not depend on the amount of the sample, therefore temperature is a(n) _____ property. In contrast, heat is a(n) _____ property, which means that the amount of energy transferred as heat depends on the amount of the sample.

4. The total energy content of a sample is its _____, and is represented by the symbol $H$.

**Complete each statement below by writing the correct term in the space provided.**

5. The SI temperature unit is _____.

6. A kelvin is the same temperature interval as a degree _____.

7. Because $0.00°C$ is equal to _____, individual temperatures have different numerical values on the two scales.

8. A temperature difference taken between two objects has _____ numerical value in Kelvins and in degrees Celsius.

9. Heat, like other forms of energy, is measured in _____.

Name _____ Class _____ Date _____

**▌Concept Review** *continued*

**10.** If the temperature of an object is found to be 73.15 K, its value in degrees

Celsius is _____.

**11.** Kelvin temperature = Celsius temperature + _____

**Solve the following problems and write your answers in the space provided.**

**12.** Calculate the energy needed to raise the temperature of 180.0 g of water from 10.0°C to 40.0°C. The molar heat capacity for water is 75.3 J/K·mol.

**13.** How many joules would be required to change the temperature of 250.0 g of aluminum from 15.0°C to 75.0°C? The molar heat capacity of aluminum is 24.2 J/K·mol.

**14.** How much energy is required to raise the temperature of 68.0 g of tin from 25.0°C to 80.0°C? The molar heat capacity of tin is 11.1 J/K·mol.

**15.** The molar heat capacity of nitrogen, $N_2$, is 29.1 J/K·mol. How much energy is required to raise the temperature of 40.5 g of nitrogen 45 K?

Skills Worksheet

# Concept Review

## Section: Using Enthalpy

**Complete each statement below by writing the correct term in the space provided.**

1. The total energy of a system is its _____,or $H$. The only

   way to measure energy is through a _____. The

   _____ enthalpy change is the enthalpy change of one

   mole of an element or compound.

2. When a pure substance is heated or cooled, but does not change state, the

   energy as heat is the _____ as the enthalpy change.

   Therefore the molar enthalpy change is equal to the _____

   _____ multiplied by the _____,or

   $\Delta H=$ _____.

3. A _____ enthalpy change means that the change requires

   energy and that the process is _____. A

   _____ enthalpy change means that the change releases

   energy or is a _____ process.

4. The science that examines the energy changes that accompany chemical and

   physical processes is called _____.

**Solve the following problems and write your answers in the space provided.**

5. How much does the molar enthalpy change when 147 g of water cools from
   90.0°C to 17.0°C? The molar heat capacity for water is 75.3 J/K·mol.

6. How much does the molar enthalpy change when 432 g of water is heated
   from 18.0°C to 71.0°C? The molar heat capacity for water is 75.3 J/K·mol.

Name _____ Class _____ Date _____

# Concept Review

## Section: Changes in Enthalpy During Chemical Reactions

**Complete each statement below by writing the correct term in the space provided.**

1. In most chemical reactions, the enthalpy change can be measured in terms of energy in the form of _____ released or gained during the reaction. A change in enthalpy in a reaction depends on many variables, but _____ is one of the most important. To standardize the enthalpies of reactions, data for _____ and _____ are presented at the standard thermodynamic temperature of _____ °C, or _____ K. When a chemical equation is used in calculating thermodynamic values, coefficients represent _____ of a substance. The enthalpy change in forming 1 mol of a substance from its elements at 298.15K is called the _____ of formation.

**Write the answers to the following questions in the space provided.**

2. Explain how the two types of calorimeters are used to measure the energy released or absorbed in a chemical reaction.

_____

_____

_____

_____

3. State Hess's law.

_____

_____

_____

_____

**| Concept Review** *continued*

## Solve the following problems and write your answers in the space provided.

**4.** What is the enthalpy change for the following reaction? Is the reaction exothermic or endothermic?

$$Cl_2(g) + 2HBr(g) \rightarrow 2HCl(g) + Br_2(g)$$

**5.** What is the enthalpy change for the following reaction? Is the reaction exothermic or endothermic?

$$CaCO_3(s) \rightarrow CaO(s) + CO_2(g)$$

Name _____ Class _____ Date _____

# Concept Review

## Section: Order and Spontaneity

**Complete each statement below by writing the correct term in the space provided.**

1. The property of a system that makes a process occur consists of two driving forces, a tendency toward the greatest _____ state and a tendency toward the lowest _____ state.

2. The quantity of entropy possessed by 1 mol of a substance is called _____.

3. The symbol for standard entropy is _____ and the units used are _____, the same as for molar heat capacity.

4. The thermodynamic quantity used to predict whether a reaction will occur spontaneously is _____ and is defined by the equation $G$ = _____.

**Complete each statement below by writing the correct term in the space provided.**

5. A reaction is more likely to occur if the change in entropy is _____.

6. The entropy of a substance _____ with temperature.

7. _____ have greater standard entropies than liquids.

8. _____ have the most freedom to move, so their standard entropies are the greatest.

9. At _____, no disorder means no entropy.

10. The entropy change of a reaction is standard entropy of the _____ minus the standard entropy of the _____.

11. Because the atoms in a diamond are in a more ordered state than in graphite, the change in entropy in changing graphite into a diamond is _____.

| Concept Review *continued*

**12.** A system with more energy has more _____.

**13.** A process is spontaneous if $\Delta G$ is _____.

**14.** All spontaneous processes occur with a _____ in Gibbs energy.

**Complete each statement below by underlining the correct word or phrase in brackets. Refer to the following two expressions when answering the items below.**

$\Delta H$ = enthalpy of products − enthalpy of reactants

$\Delta G = \Delta H - T\Delta S$

**15.** The products of an [endothermic, exothermic] reaction have an energy higher than that of the reactants.

**16.** In endothermic reactions, $\Delta H$ has a [positive, negative] value.

**17.** The drive to achieve a state of [minimum, maximum] Gibbs energy may be interpreted as the driving force of a chemical reaction.

**18.** A chemical reaction occurs if it is accompanied by a(n) [increase, decrease] in Gibbs energy.

**19.** If $\Delta G$ is negative, $-\Delta G$, the reaction is [spontaneous, nonspontaneous].

**20.** The expression for $\Delta G$ shows that when $\Delta H$ is negative and $\Delta S$ is positive, $\Delta G$ is [positive, negative]. Thus, [endothermic, exothermic] reactions, which are accompanied by a(n) [increase, decrease] in entropy of the system, are probable.

**21.** The expression for $\Delta G$ shows that when $\Delta H$ is positive and $\Delta S$ is negative, $\Delta G$ is [positive, negative]. This means that [endothermic, exothermic] reactions accompanied by a(n) [increase, decrease] in entropy are improbable.

**22.** At very high temperatures, the sign and magnitude of $\Delta G$ and the spontaneity of a reaction are determined primarily by the change in [enthalpy, entropy].

**23.** According to the expression for $\Delta G$, the [higher, lower] the temperature for a positive entropy change, the greater the chances are that the reaction will be spontaneous.

**24.** When the temperature of a system is low, the product $T\Delta S$ is very [small, large] compared to the $\Delta H$ term and has little influence on the value of $\Delta G$. In such cases, the reaction may occur as the [enthalpy, entropy] change predicts.

**Solve the following problems and write your answers in the space provided.**

**25.** What is the entropy change for the following reaction?

$$Ca(s) + 2H_2O(l) \rightarrow Ca(OH)_2(s) + H_2(g)$$

**26.** What is the entropy change for the following reaction?

$$4HBr(g) + O_2(g) \rightarrow 2H_2O(l) + 2Br_2(l)$$

**27.** Calculate the change in Gibbs energy for the following reaction at 25°C. Is the reaction spontaneous?

$$2H_2O_2(l) \rightarrow 2H_2O(l) + O_2(g)$$

**28.** Calculate the change in Gibbs energy for the given reaction at 25°C. Is the reaction spontaneous?

$$CaCO_3(s) \rightarrow CaO(s) + CO_2(g)$$

Name _____ Class _____ Date _____

# Concept Review

## Section: States and State Changes

**Complete each statement below by choosing a term from the following list. Use each term only once.**

| | | | |
|---|---|---|---|
| solid | cohesion | melting | surface tension |
| liquid | adhesion | evaporation | boiling point |
| gas | deposition | condensation | melting point |
| viscous | freezing | sublimation | freezing point |

**1.** The particles in a _____ are very close together in an orderly, fixed, and usually crystalline arrangement. _____ is an endothermic change of state in which a solid becomes a liquid. The temperature and pressure at which a solid becomes a liquid is its _____.

**2.** Because particles in a _____ have enough kinetic energy to be able to move past each other easily, they take the shape of their container. While many liquids flow readily, many are resistant to flowing, or are

_____.

**3.** Because they are held close together, liquid particles are more affected by forces between particles. They have attraction for each other, or

_____, as well as attraction for particles of solid surfaces, called

_____. Liquids tend to form spherical drops because of

_____, or the tendency to decrease their surface area to the smallest size possible, thereby decreasing their energy. Particles in a liquid can gain enough kinetic energy to leave the surface and become a gas in a

process called _____.

**4.** Attractive forces between _____ particles do not have a great effect, which makes the particles essentially independent of each other. The temperature and pressure at which the number of liquid particles becoming gas particles is the same as the number of gas particles returning to the liquid

phase is called a substance's _____. Gas particles lose energy and

become liquid during _____.

**5.** The process during which a liquid substance loses energy and becomes a

solid is called _____. The temperature at which this change

occurs is the _____ for a substance.

**6.** The particles of solids may become gas particles without first melting in a

process called _____. The reverse of this process, in which a gas

becomes a solid without first becoming liquid, is called _____.

Skills Worksheet

# Concept Review

## Section: Intermolecular Forces

**Write the answers to the following questions in the space provided.**

1. Why do ionic compounds tend to have higher boiling and melting points than molecular compounds have?

   _____

   _____

   _____

   _____

2. Why do molecular substances with weak intermolecular forces have low melting points?

   _____

   _____

   _____

3. Why do molecular substances with strong intermolecular forces have high melting points?

   _____

   _____

   _____

   _____

4. How do dipole-dipole forces affect the melting and boiling points of substances?

   _____

   _____

   _____

   _____

   _____

**Concept Review** *continued*

**5.** What forces are involved in hydrogen bonding?

_____

_____

_____

_____

**6.** What effect does hydrogen bonding have on the physical properties of water?

_____

_____

_____

_____

_____

**7.** How can a molecule have a momentary dipole?

_____

_____

_____

**8.** Name the force of attraction between molecules with momentary dipoles.

_____

**9.** How do London forces and dipole-dipole forces between molecules differ from forces between ions in crystals?

_____

_____

_____

**10.** Explain the role of particle size and shape on the strength of attractive forces.

_____

_____

_____

_____

Name _____ Class _____ Date _____

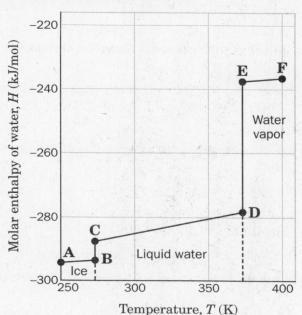

Skills Worksheet

# Concept Review

## Section: Energy of State Changes

Complete each statement below by writing the correct word or words in the space provided. Refer to Figure 1, below, to answer items 1–6.

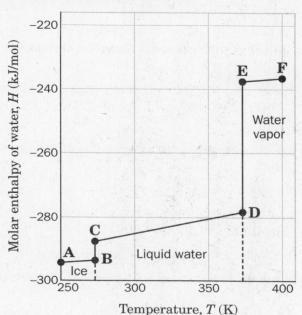

**Figure 1**

**1.** The molar enthalpy change at 273.15 K (B → C) is called the

_____

**2.** The molar enthalpy change at 373.15 K (D → E) is called the

_____

**3.** The slopes of the slowly rising lines in the graph, A → B, C → D, and E → F, are the _____ of water at each state.

**4.** The large heat capacity of liquid water is attributed to _____

## Solve the following problem and write your answer in the space provided.

**5.** The enthalpy of vaporization for nitric acid is 30.30 kJ/mol, and the molar entropy of vaporization is 84.4 J/mol·K. Calculate the boiling point of nitric acid.

# Concept Review *continued*

**Complete each statement below by circling the correct word or phrase in brackets.**

6. It takes a lot [more, less] heat to vaporize the water than to melt ice.

7. Heat must be [absorbed, released] to raise the temperature of ice, water, or water vapor.

8. The enthalpy changes accompanying a change of state are much [smaller, greater] than those that accompany the heating of the substance at each state.

9. The tendency to [lower, higher] energy is seen in thermodynamics as positive $\Delta H$ values, and a(n) [increase, decrease] in disorder is seen as negative $\Delta S$ values.

10. During changes of state, changes in enthalpy and entropy [oppose, complement] each other. The relative values of $\Delta H$ and $T\Delta S$ determine which state is preferred.

11. During evaporation, a liquid becomes a gas at a temperature [at, well below] its boiling point.

12. Evaporation is a [endothermic, exothermic] process.

13. Gibbs energy relates entropy and enthalpy changes to the [spontaneity, rate] of a phase transition.

14. A process is spontaneous if $\Delta G$ is [positive, negative].

15. All spontaneous processes occur with a(n) [increase, decrease] in Gibbs energy.

16. When $\Delta G$ is exactly zero, the system is in a state of [flux, equilibrium].

17. The melting point of a solid equals the enthalpy of fusion [divided, multiplied] by the entropy of fusion.

18. Boiling occurs when the tendency toward [order, disorder] overcomes the tendency to lose energy.

19. [Condensation, evaporation] occurs when the tendency to lose energy overcomes the tendency to increase disorder.

20. Boiling points are pressure dependent because pressure has [no, a large] effect on the entropy of a gas.

Skills Worksheet

# Concept Review

## Section: Phase Equilibrium

**Complete each statement below by choosing a term from the following list. Use each term only once.**

| | | | |
|---|---|---|---|
| phase | triple point | vapor pressure | normal boiling point |
| equilibrium | critical point | phase diagram | supercritical fluid |

**1.** A _____ is a region that has the same composition and properties throughout. When particles are constantly moving between two or more phases, yet no net change in the amount of substance in either phase occurs,

the system is said to be in _____. The pressure exerted by the molecules of a gas, or vapor, in equilibrium with a liquid is called the

_____. When you increase a system's temperature to the point at which the vapor pressure of a substance is equal to standard atmospheric

pressure, you have reached the substance's _____.

**2.** A graph of the relationship between the physical state of a substance and the

temperature and pressure of the substance is called a _____. The temperature and pressure conditions at which the solid, liquid, and gaseous

phases of a substance coexist at equilibrium is called the _____. The temperature and pressure at which the gas and liquid states of a

substance become identical and form one phase is the _____.

Above this temperature, the substance is referred to as a _____, and the liquid and vapor phases are indistinguishable.

**Write the answer to the following questions in the space provided.**

**3.** What physical factor does the average kinetic energy of molecules depend on?

_____

_____

**4.** Explain why the vapor pressure of molecules doubles or triples for every 10°C increase in temperature, while the kinetic energy increases only about 3%.

_____

_____

_____

**5.** Use the phase diagram for water in your text to complete the table below and items 6–8.

| Description of point | Temperature | Pressure | Point |
|---|---|---|---|
| The temperature and pressure at which three phases of water exist in equilibrium | | | |
| The temperature at which water boils at 1.0 atm of pressure | | | |
| The temperature at which water freezes/melts at 1.0 atm of pressure | | | |
| The temperature and pressure at and above which the properties of water vapor cannot be distinguished from those of liquid water—water exists as a single phase | | | |

**Write the answer to the following questions in the space provided.**

**6.** Name the phases that water will exhibit if the pressure is kept constant at 110 kPa and the temperature is gradually increased from −10°C to 110°C.

_____

**7.** Name the phases that water will exhibit if the pressure is kept constant at 0.31 kPa and the temperature is gradually increased from −10°C to 110°C. What term is given to the phase transformation of water that occurs under these conditions?

_____

**8.** Along which line segment do solids and liquids coexist? Describe the slope of this line for water. What will an increase in pressure do to water's melting point?

_____

_____

_____

Skills Worksheet

# Concept Review

## Section: Characteristics of Gases

**Complete each statement below by underlining the correct word or phrase in brackets.**

1. Gases have unique properties because the distance between gas particles is much [greater than, smaller than] the particles of a liquid or a solid. In contrast to solids and liquids, gases [partially, completely] fill their containers.

2. Gases are considered [liquids, fluids] because their particles [can, cannot] move past each other easily and are thus able to flow. Gas particles can be forced closer together by applying pressure to them, thus [decreasing, increasing] their volume.

3. Gases have much [higher, lower] densities than do liquids and solids. Because of the [large, small] distance between gas particles, much of the space occupied by a gas is [vibrating, empty].

4. According to the kinetic-molecular theory, gas particles travel relatively [long, short] distances before colliding with each other. These collisions with each other and with the walls of their container result in [pressure, fluid]. These collisions are perfectly elastic; that is, energy is [completely, inversely] transferred from one particle to another.

5. Although gases [are, are not] dense, they [do, do not] have mass, therefore in a gravitational field they also [have, do not have] weight. As gas particles are attracted by Earth's gravity, they collide with each other and with Earth's surface, creating [the atmosphere, air pressure]. Pressure is the amount of force exerted per unit area of [volume, surface].

6. Air is [less dense, denser] as you move closer to Earth's surface because the weight of atmospheric gases at any elevation compresses the gases below them. At high altitudes, less dense air exerts [more, less] pressure.

7. The kinetic-molecular theory states that particles of matter are in constant rapid, random motion. The average kinetic energy of random motion is [proportional, inversely proportional] to temperature in kelvins. This means that heat [decreases, increases] the energy of random motion of a gas.

## Concept Review *continued*

**In the space provided, write the letter of the description that best matches the term or phrase.**

_____ **8.** pressure

_____ **9.** newton (N)

_____ **10.** pascal (Pa)

_____ **11.** one standard atmosphere (atm)

_____ **12.** standard temperature and pressure (STP)

**a.** the force that will increase the speed of a 1 kg mass by 1 m/s each second that the force is applied

**b.** a unit of pressure equal to a force of 1 N on an area of 1 m$^2$

**c.** force exerted per unit area

**d.** at sea level, the pressure necessary to maintain a mercury column in a barometer at a height of 760 mm

**e.** standard conditions for a gas at 0°C and 1 atm

**Solve the following problem and write your answer in the space provided.**

**13.** Convert the pressure of 750 mm Hg to atmospheres.

Skills Worksheet

# Concept Review

## Section: The Gas Laws

**Refer to Figure 1, below, to complete items 1–5. Assume the gas in the cylinder is at constant temperature.**

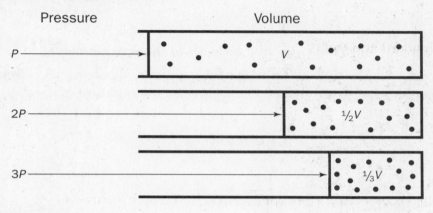

**Figure 1**

**1.** In general, as the pressure increases, the volume _____, and as

the pressure decreases, the volume _____.

**2.** Name and state the law that describes the behavior of the gas in the cylinder.

_____

_____

_____

**3.** Complete the table, given the initial pressure and volume of the gas in the cylinder.

| Pressure (kPa) | Volume (L) | Pressure × Volume, *PV* |
|---|---|---|
| 100 | 0.500 | |
| 200 | | |
| | 0.167 | |

**4.** The data in item 3 show that the _____ of the pressure times the volume of a given sample of gas at constant temperature is a(n)

_____. The equation that expresses this relationship is

_____ and is known as _____.

**Concept Review** *continued*

**5.** The data in item 3, on the previous page, also show that if the product, $PV$, is measured for a given quantity of gas at one set of conditions, $P_1V_1$, and then at another set of conditions, $P_2V_2$, both products are found to be _____ to the constant _____ Using this information, provide an alternate way to express Boyle's law.

_____

**Solve the following problems and write your answers in the space provided.**

**6.** A sample of gas occupies 20 L under a pressure of 1 atm. What will its volume be if the pressure is increased to 2 atm? Assume the temperature of the gas sample does not change.

**7.** A sample of oxygen occupies 10.0 L under a pressure of 105 kPa. At what pressure will it occupy 13.4 L if the temperature does not change?

**8.** A student collects 400 mL of oxygen at 9.80 kPa. If the temperature remains constant, what volume would this gas occupy at 9.40 kPa?

| Concept Review *continued*

**Answer the following items in the space provided. Refer to Figure 2, below.
Assume the gas in the cylinder is at constant pressure.**

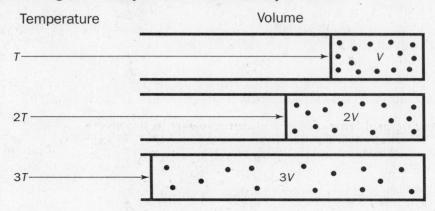

**Figure 2**

9. In general, as the temperature increases, the volume _____, and

   as the temperature decreases, the volume _____.

10. Name and state the law that describes the behavior of the gas in the cylinder.

    _____

    _____

    _____

11. Complete the table, given the initial pressure and volume of the gas in the
    cylinder.

| Temperature (K) | Volume (mL) | Volume/Temperature, *V/T* |
|:---:|:---:|:---:|
| 100 | 199 | |
| | 402 | 2.01 |
| 300 | | |

12. The data in item 11 show that the volume of a given sample of gas divided by

    its absolute temperature, _____, is a(n) _____. The

    equation that expresses this relationship is _____ and is known as

    _____.

Gases

| Concept Review *continued*

**13.** The data in item 11 also show that the ratio, *V/T*, for the same gas sample at any set of volume-temperature conditions (at constant pressure) will always

_____ the same constant, _____. Using this information, provide an alternate way to express Charles's law.

_____

**14.** How does a change in temperature affect the pressure of a gas when its volume is kept constant? Use equations to express this relationship when more than one set of pressure-temperature conditions are applied to the same gas sample at a fixed volume.

_____

_____

_____

**Solve the following problems and write your answers in the space provided.**

**15.** What is the volume of a gas at 253 K if the gas occupies 50.0 mL at a temperature of 273 K? Volume and mass are held constant.

**16.** A gas at 300 K exerts a pressure of 99 kPa. What pressure is exerted by the same gas at 273 K? Volume and mass are held constant.

**17.** A gas occupies 50.0 mL at standard temperature. What volume will it occupy at 335°C with the pressure unchanged? (Be sure to convert the Celsius temperature to kelvins.)

Skills Worksheet

# Concept Review

## Section: Molecular Composition of Gases

**In the space provided, write the letter of the description that best matches the term or phrase.**

_____ **1.** Avogadro's law

_____ **2.** Gay-Lussac's law of combining volumes

_____ **3.** effusion

_____ **4.** diffusion

_____ **5.** Graham's law of diffusion

**a.** the passage of a gas through a small opening

**b.** At constant temperature and pressure, gases react in volume proportions that are whole numbers (equivalent to the coefficients in the balanced chemical equation).

**c.** Equal volumes of different gases under the same conditions of temperature and pressure have the same number of molecules.

**d.** the process by which particles mix by dispersing from regions of higher concentration to regions of lower concentration

**e.** The rates of diffusion for two gases are inversely proportional to the square roots of their molar masses at the same temperature and pressure.

**Solve the following problems and write your answers in the space provided.**

**6.** Assume 5 mol of $N_2$ gas is confined in a 10 L container at 523 K. Calculate the pressure of the gas in kilopascals and in atmospheres.

**Concept Review** *continued*

7. If 44 g of a gas is found to have a volume of 24.5 L under a pressure of 50.66 kPa at 298 K, what is the molar mass of the gas?

8. A 20 L vessel contains a gas under a pressure of 5 atm at 303 K. How many moles of gas are in the vessel?

9. The volume of a gas is 20.0 mL under a pressure of 97.3 kPa and at a temperature of 297 K. What would the volume be if it were measured under 95.7 kPa and at 286 K?

10. Given 20.0 L of ammonia at 278 K and 101.325 kPa, determine its volume at 303 K and 1.05 atm.

**Concept Review** *continued*

**11.** In **Figure 3,** below, $NH_3$ gas from a concentrated ammonia-water solution reacts with HCl gas from a concentrated hydrochloric acid solution to produce a white cloud of solid $NH_4Cl$. Does the cloud form near *A*, *B*, or *C*? Use Graham's law of diffusion to verify your answer.

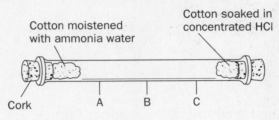

Cotton moistened with ammonia water

Cotton soaked in concentrated HCl

Cork       A       B       C

**Figure 3**

_____

_____

_____

**12.** Compare the speed of effusion of $H_2(g)$ with that of $Br_2(g)$ under the same conditions.

**13.** Under constant pressure, a small basketball pump is filled with helium, He, gas; the helium is then forced out of a small aperture in 2 seconds. The same pump is filled with hydrogen bromide, HBr, gas. Under the same pressure, how long will it take to force this gas out?

**Concept Review** *continued*

**14.** If 200 mL of hydrogen diffuses through a porous container four times as rapidly as an unknown gas, calculate the molar mass of the unknown gas.

**15.** Determine the total pressure of the gases in **Figure 4,** below.

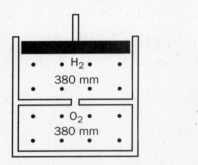 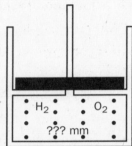

Partial Pressure of $H_2$ + Partial Pressure of $O_2$ = Total Pressure

**Figure 4**

**16.** Use Gay-Lussac's law of combining volumes to determine the volumes of the reacting gases in the following equations:

$$N_2(g) + 3H_2(g) \rightarrow 2NH_3(g)$$

_____ volume + _____ volumes → _____ volumes

$$4NH_3(g) + 5O_2(g) \rightarrow 4NO(g) + 6H_2O(g)$$

_____ volume + _____ volumes → _____ volumes + _____ volumes

**17.** The equation for the complete combustion of carbon is as follows:

$$C(s) + O_2(g) \rightarrow CO_2(g)$$

What volume of $CO_2$ is produced when 24.0 g of C is burned at a pressure of 99.3 kPa and at 298 K?

**Concept Review** *continued*

**18.** Calculate the volume of $H_2$ produced at 300 K and 98.65 kPa when 48 g of Mg reacts with excess HCl according to the following equation:

$$Mg(s) + 2HCl(aq) \rightarrow MgCl(aq) + H_2(g)$$

**19.** The equation for the reaction of sodium with water is as follows:

$$2Na(s) + 2H_2O(l) \rightarrow H_2(g) + 2NaOH(aq)$$

How many liters of $H_2$ are produced when 12.0 g of Na reacts with $H_2O$ at 293 K and 99.3 kPa?

Name _____ Class _____ Date _____

# Concept Review

## Section: What Is a Solution?

In the space provided, write the letter of the description that best matches the term or phrase.

_____ 1. suspension

_____ 2. colloid

_____ 3. solution

_____ 4. solvent

_____ 5. solute

_____ 6. aqueous

**a.** in a solution, the substance in which the solute is dissolved

**b.** describes a solution in which the solvent is water

**c.** a mixture in which large particles are temporarily suspended throughout a liquid or gas

**d.** in a solution, the substance dissolved in the solvent

**e.** a stable, homogeneous mixture

**f.** a mixture of very small particles stably suspended in liquid, solid, or gas

Mark each mixture below *H* if it is homogeneous and *Ht* if it is heterogeneous

_____ 7. milk

_____ 8. gasoline

_____ 9. muddy water

_____ 10. steel

_____ 11. coffee

_____ 12. ink

_____ 13. crude oil

_____ 14. bronze

_____ 15. brass

_____ 16. sea water

Complete each statement with the correct term or phrase.

17. All parts of a _____ mixture have the same composition.

18. _____ mixtures are not uniform in composition.

19. A true solution is formed when a solute, as molecules or ions, is dispersed

   throughout a _____ to form a homogeneous mixture.

20. A true solution consists of a single _____ .

**Concept Review** *continued*

**21.** Any mixture that is heterogeneous on a microscopic level is a

_____.

**22.** A _____ is a mixture in which particles of the mixture are more or

less evenly dispersed throughout a liquid or gas.

**23.** _____ are intermediate between suspensions and solutions.

**24.** To _____ a mixture, simply pour the liquids off and leave the
settled solids behind.

**25.** A centrifuge separates mixtures into components that have different

_____.

**26.** The force created by a centrifuge pushes denser substances to the

_____ of the tube.

**27.** During _____, liquid and solid particles smaller than the holes in
filter paper pass through the filter paper and form a filtrate.

**28.** Paper chromatography employs _____, the attraction of the
surface of a liquid to the surface of a solid.

**29.** Dyes with the _____ attraction for the paper travel fastest and
farthest during paper chromatography.

**30.** Distillation separates the components of a mixture based on their

_____ points.

**31.** During distillation, as one component reaches its boiling point, its

_____ is removed and allowed to cool and condense.

**32.** Crude oil is separated into _____ by distillation.

Skills Worksheet

# Concept Review

## Section: Concentration and Molarity

**Complete each statement below by choosing a term from the following list.**
**Use each term only once.**

| | | | | |
|---|---|---|---|---|
| concentration | moles | solute | solution | liter |
| parts per million | molality | molarity | ratios | |

1. _____ is the quantity of solute in a specific quantity of solvent or

   solution. One way of expressing concentration is to use the unit of measure

   called _____; it is the ratio of _____ amount (in

   moles) to _____ volume (in liters), or simply _____ of

   solute per L of solution. Table 1 in your textbook lists other concentration

   units or_____, such as _____ ($m$ = mol solute/kg

   solvent) and_____ (ppm = mL solute/1 000 000.0 mL solution).

**Solve the following problems and write your answer in the space provided.**

2. What is the molarity of a hydrochloric acid solution that has a volume of 1500
   mL and contains 441 g of HCl?

3. What is the molarity of a sugar solution that has a volume of 0.500 L and
   contains 17.1 g of ordinary sugar ($C_{12}H_{22}O_{11}$)?

| Concept Review *continued*

4. What is the mass in grams of $BaCl_2$ that is needed to prepare 200 mL of a 0.500 M solution?

5. What volume in liters of a 0.200 M solution of silver nitrate, $AgNO_3$, would be needed to react with an excess of calcium chloride, $CaCl_2$, to provide 5.74 g of silver chloride, AgCl?

$$2AgNO_3(aq) + CaCl_2\ (aq) \rightarrow 2AgCl(s) + Ca(NO_3)_2(aq)$$

6. What mass in grams of $PbI_2$ would be formed if 0.500 L of 0.100 M $Pb(NO_3)_2$ reacts with an excess of KI solution according to the following equation?

$$Pb(NO_3)_2(aq) + 2KI(aq) \rightarrow PbI_2(s) + 2KNO_3(aq)$$

Skills Worksheet

# Concept Review

## Section: Solubility and the Dissolving Process

**Complete each statement below by underlining the correct word or phrase in brackets.**

1. Two liquids that are soluble in each other in all proportions are said to be [miscible, immiscible].

2. Whether A dissolves in B depends on a [imbalance, balance] between favorable entropy and favorable enthalpy.

3. Two compounds that are both polar or both nonpolar are likely to be [immiscible, miscible].

4. Two compounds that can form hydrogen bonds with each other are likely to be [immiscible, miscible].

**Complete each statement below by choosing a term from the following list. Use each term only once.**

| | | | |
|---|---|---|---|
| Henry's law | solubility | maximum | solvent |
| solution | saturated | decreases | supersaturated |
| miscibility | equilibrium | solute | pressure |

5. A(n) _____ is a homogeneous mixture of two or more substances.

   The dissolving medium is called the _____. The substance

   dissolved in a solution is called the _____.

6. The _____ of a solute is defined as the _____ amount of that solute that will dissolve in a given amount of a solvent under specified conditions.

7. A(n) _____ solution cannot dissolve any more solute under the given conditions.

8. According to _____, the solubility of a gas in a liquid is directly

   proportional to the partial _____ of the gas above the liquid.

9. The solubility of a gas _____ as the solvent's temperature increases.

10. A(n)_____ solution contains more than the amount of solute specified by the solubility at a given set of conditions.

11. Solubility _____ is the physical state in which the opposing processes of dissolution and crystallization of a solute occur at equal rates.

12. Hydrogen bonds explain in part the abnormally high boiling point of water

   and the complete _____ of water and ethylene glycol.

**In the space provided, write the letter of the term or phrase that best completes each statement or best answers each question.**

_____13. Fats, greases, and oils are difficult to remove from fabrics by simple washing because they are
   **a.** polar.
   **b.** nonpolar.
   **c.** miscible.
   **d.** soluble.

_____14. Nonpolar solvents will dissolve materials that are themselves
   **a.** nonpolar.
   **b.** polar.
   **c.** insoluble.
   **d.** None of the above

_____15. The best dry-cleaning fluid to remove a polar stain from fabric would most likely be a
   **a.** polar liquid solvent.
   **b.** polar liquid solute.
   **c.** nonpolar liquid solvent.
   **d.** nonpolar liquid solute.

_____16. Vitamin C is easily transported by the blood and easily excreted by the kidneys because it
   **a.** is immiscible.
   **b.** forms a suspension.
   **c.** is water-soluble.
   **d.** forms a precipitate.

_____17. It is possible to take too much vitamin A but not vitamin C because
   **a.** vitamin A is water soluble.
   **b.** vitamin C is fat soluble.
   **c.** vitamin A is fat soluble and builds up in body fat.
   **d.** the kidneys are less effective at processing small, water-soluble molecules.

**| Concept Review** *continued*

## Complete each statement below by underlining the correct word or phrase in brackets.

**18.** [Distillation, Dissociation] occurs when ions separate from the crystals of ionic compounds during the solution process.

**19.** [Hydration, Dissociation] occurs when water molecules attach themselves to the ions of the solute during the solution process.

**20.** For the aqueous ionic solution represented by the equation $NaCl(s) \rightarrow Na^+(aq) + Cl^-(aq)$, how does the tendency toward minimum energy compare with the tendency toward maximum entropy? They are [equal, unequal].

**21.** Though [easy, difficult] to predict, the solubilities of ionic compounds are quite [easy, difficult] to measure.

**22.** [All, Few] compounds containing nitrate ions or ammonium ions are [soluble, insoluble] in water.

**23.** Unlike the solubility of gases, the solubility of most ionic compounds [increases, decreases] with temperature.

**24.** In a saturated solution, some excess solute remains, and the amount that dissolves is [equal, unequal] to the solubility value for that temperature. Some supersaturated solutions are able to contain [more, less] than the solubility indicates would normally be possible as long as [there is no excess, there is an excess] of undissolved solute remaining.

Skills Worksheet

# Concept Review

## Section: Physical Properties of Solutions

**Write the answer to the following questions in the space provided.**

1. Separately, neither NaCl nor $H_2O$ can conduct electricity, but if you put them together in the form of an aqueous solution, you have a conductor. Explain why.

_____

_____

_____

2. Explain why you should not seek shelter under a tree during a thunderstorm.

_____

_____

_____

_____

**In the space provided, write the letter of the term or phrase that best completes each statement or best answers each question.**

_____ 3. What term best describes a material's ability to conduct electricity?
   **a.** electrolysis
   **b.** electrolytic
   **c.** conductivity
   **d.** resistivity

_____ 4. What term best describes the ability of pure water to conduct an electric current?
   **a.** nonconductor
   **b.** conductor
   **c.** electrolyte
   **d.** electrolysis

_____ 5. What do we call a solute whose water solution conducts electricity?
   **a.** nonconductor
   **b.** electrolyte
   **c.** nonelectrolyte
   **d.** aqueous

_____ **6.** Which is a molecular substance whose water solution conducts electricity?
  **a.** liquid hydrogen
  **b.** iron
  **c.** sugar
  **d.** hydrogen chloride

_____ **7.** What happens when acetic acid dissolves in water?
  **a.** Hydronium ions are one of the products.
  **b.** The resulting solution will conduct electricity.
  **c.** Most of the acid remains as un-ionized molecules in equilibrium with ions.
  **d.** All of the above

_____ **8.** Which of the following types of water does not conduct electricity?
  **a.** chlorinated water
  **b.** ground water
  **c.** saltwater
  **d.** distilled water

**Complete each statement below by choosing a term from the following list. Use each term only once.**

| | | |
|---|---|---|
| vapor pressure | total number | reduced |
| solute | less | colligative |
| decrease | increase | nature |
| freezing-point depression | particles | concentration |
| boiling-point elevation | properties | greater |

**9.** The addition of a(n) _____ to a pure liquid solvent changes the

_____ of the liquid. The vapor pressure, boiling point, and freezing

point of a solution are _____ properties and depend upon the

_____ of solute particles rather than on their _____.

**10.** The _____ of a liquid is related to the tendency of the molecules

to escape from a solution. For example, the proportion and escaping tendency

of water molecules is _____ when a solute is dissolved in pure

water, and the vapor pressure of the solution is therefore _____

than that of pure water.

**11.** Decreasing the vapor pressure of a solvent by the addition of a solute causes

a(n) _____ in the boiling point, a(n) _____.

**12.** The decrease in the vapor pressure of a solvent resulting from the addition of

a solute causes a corresponding _____ in its freezing point, a

_____.

**13.** The _____ of the solute affect(s) freezing- and boiling-point

changes. The more _____, the _____ the freezing-

point depression and boiling-point elevation.

**Complete each statement below by underlining the correct word or phrase in brackets.**

**14.** The droplets formed in an [suspension, emulsion] are colloid-size particles.

**15.** A [salt, soap] ion has a polar end and a nonpolar end.

**16.** Soap exhibits the characteristic property of a [suspension, surfactant] in that it forms a layer between two dissimilar phases.

**17.** [Hard, Soft] water enhances the surfactant abilities of soap.

**18.** [Detergents, Colloids] outperform soaps in hard water.

**In the space provided, write the letter of the description that best matches the term or phrase.**

_____**19.** soap

_____**20.** surfactant

_____**21.** emulsion

_____**22.** synthetic detergent

_____**23.** hard water

**a.** a class of salts that concentrate at the boundary between two immiscible phases

**b.** any mixture of two or more immiscible liquids in which one liquid is dispersed in the other

**c.** a sodium or potassium salt of a fatty acid with a long hydrocarbon chain

**d.** can be used in hard water without forming precipitates

**e.** contains insoluble ions such as calcium or magnesium

Name _____ Class _____ Date _____

# Concept Review

## Section: Reversible Reactions and Equilibrium

**Answer the following questions in the space provided.**

1. What is the difference between a reversible reaction and one that goes to completion?

_____

_____

_____

_____

2. When is chemical equilibrium reached?

_____

_____

_____

_____

3. What do the arrows in this equation indicate: $A \rightleftharpoons B$?

_____

_____

4. What is a complex ion?

_____

_____

_____

5. What is dynamic equilibrium?

_____

_____

_____

# Concept Review *continued*

**Mark each statement below *R* if it describes a reversible reaction and *C* if it describes a reaction that goes to completion.**

_____ **6.** When an automobile battery is used for power, chemicals are consumed in the process of furnishing electricity. When the battery is recharged, the original chemicals are regenerated

_____ **7.** A reaction between solutions of sodium chloride and silver nitrate produces an insoluble white precipitate, silver chloride.

_____ **8.** In the reaction between hydrochloric acid and potassium hydroxide, water is practically un-ionized.

_____ **9.** Salt crystals in a saturated solution demonstrate crystal growth.

**Refer to Figure 1 to answer items 10–12. Complete each statement below by circling the correct term.**

**10.** Initially, the concentration of each product, C and D, is [0, < 0], and the rate of the reverse reaction is [0, > 0]. At the same time, the concentration of each reactant, A and B, is at a [minimum, maximum], and the rate of the forward reaction is the [minimum, maximum] rate.

**11.** The rate of the forward reaction [increases, decreases] as reactants are used up.

**12.** The rate of the reverse reaction [increases, decreases] until finally, at time [$t_0$, $t_1$] the rates become equal, and the system reaches [completion, equilibrium].

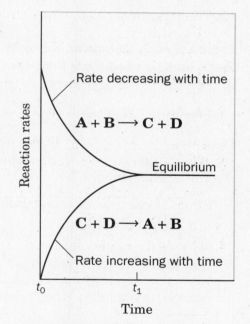

**Figure 1** Reaction rates are for the hypothetical equilibrium reaction system A + B $\rightleftarrows$ C + D. The rate of the forward reaction is represented by curve A + B. Curve C + D represents the rate of the reverse.

**Circle the letter of the choice that correctly answers the question. More than one response may be correct.**

**13.** Which of the following describes what happens at chemical equilibrium?

**a.** A dynamic state exists.

**b.** The reactions do not stop but maintain a constant concentration, or ratio, of reactants to products.

**c.** There is no net change.

**d.** Opposing chemical reactions occur at equal rates.

**Concept Review** *continued*

14. Starting with A + B, what happens in the equilibrium reaction, A + B $\rightleftarrows$ C + D?

   **a.** The speed of the forward reaction increases as A and B are used up.

   **b.** The speed of the reverse reaction increases as A and B are used up.

   **c.** The speed of the forward reaction decreases as A and B are used up.

   **d.** The speeds of both forward and reverse reactions become equal.

15. What happens in a system in which the forward reaction runs well toward completion before the speed of the reverse reaction is high enough to estab-lish equilibrium?

   **a.** the products of the reverse reaction are favored

   **b.** the products of the forward reaction are favored

   **c.** neither set of products is favored

   **d.** both reactants and products exist in equal quantities

**Complete each statement below by choosing a term from the following list. Terms may be used more than once.**

$[CoCl_4]^{2-}$     $[Co(H_2O)_6]^{2+}$   metal   $CoCl_2$        reverse      copper

complex ion   ligands        colored   $[Cu(NH_3)_4]^{2+}$   ammonia

16. A(n) _____ has a structure in which a central _____

atom or ion is bonded to more than one atom or molecule. Many complex ions

formed from transition metals are _____, and their reactions can be

tracked by color changes. For example, a weather indicator that contains a

solution of cobalt(II) chloride, _____, changes color in response to

changes in humidity. When humidity is high, $[CoCl_4]^{2-}$ reacts with water vapor

in the air and forms a pink complex ion that has six water molecules bonded to

cobalt, _____. When moisture in the air is low, the _____

reaction is favored, and a deep blue _____ forms.

Skills Worksheet

# Concept Review

## Section: Systems at Equilibrium

**Answer the following item in the space provided.**

1. Define the term equilibrium constant, $K_{eq}$.

_____

_____

_____

**Circle the term or phrase in the brackets that best completes each sentence.**

2. The [molarity constant, equilibrium constant], $K_{eq}$, has a unique value for each equilibrium system at a specific temperature.

3. We can assume that pure solids and pure liquids are [important, not important] to equilibrium systems because they do not appear in the equilibrium expression.

4. Changing the temperature of an equilibrium system [does not change, changes] both the concentration of the participants and the value of $K_{eq}$.

5. At constant temperature, changing the equilibrium concentrations [does, does not] affect $K_{eq}$. When the concentration of one of the participants is changed, the concentration of the others varies in a way that maintains a constant value for $K_{eq}$.

**Complete each statement below by writing the correct term from the following list.**

$$K_{eq} = 1 \qquad\qquad K_{eq} > 1 \qquad\qquad K_{eq} < 1$$

6. If _____, reactants of the forward reaction are favored; the forward reaction occurs only very slightly before equilibrium is established.

7. If _____, the products of the concentrations in the numerator and denominator have the same value.

8. If _____, products of the forward reaction are favored; a large value indicates an equilibrium in which the original reactants are largely converted to products.

| **Concept Review** *continued*

**Answer the following items in the space provided.**

**9.** What is the $K_{eq}$ value for the following reaction at equilibrium at a temperature of 298 K if the concentrations (in mol/L) of the reactants and products are $[N_2O_4] = 0.0450$ and $[NO_2] = 0.0161$?

$$N_2O_4(g) \rightleftarrows 2NO_2(g)$$

**10.** What is the $K_{eq}$ value for the following reaction if the equilibrium concentrations at 721 K are $[H_2] = 0.46$, $[I_2] = 0.39$, and $[HI] = 3.0$?

$$H_2(g) + I_2(g) \rightleftarrows 2HI(g)$$

**11.** What is the $K_{eq}$ value for the following reaction if the gaseous mixture in a 4 L container reaches equilibrium at 1000 K and contains 4.0 mol of $N_2$, 6.4 mol of $H_2$, and 0.40 mol of $NH_3$?

$$N_2(g) + 3H_2(g) \rightleftarrows 2NH_3(g)$$

**12.** At 328 K, the $K_{eq}$ for the reaction $2NO_2(g) \rightleftarrows N_2O_4(g)$ is 1.5. Calculate the concentration of $N_2O_4$ present in equilibrium when $[NO_2] = 0.50$.

**Concept Review** *continued*

**13.** Under a given set of conditions, an equilibrium mixture in a 1.00 L container was found to contain 0.009 98 mol HI and 0.000 867 mol $H_2$. $K_{eq}$ for the equilibrium reaction is 43.5. Calculate the concentration of $I_2$ present at equilibrium.

$$H_2(g) + I_2(g) \rightleftarrows 2HI(g)$$

**14.** Quantities of $PCl_3$ and $Cl_2$ were placed in a reaction chamber and heated to 503 K at 1 atm. At equilibrium, $K_{eq} = 0.0205$; and $[PCl_5] = 0.235$ and $[PCl_3] = 0.174$. Calculate the concentration of $Cl_2$.

$$PCl_5(g) \rightleftarrows PCl_3(g) + Cl_2(g)$$

**15.** Consider a slightly soluble salt with the general formula AaBb. The equilibrium system in a saturated solution of the salt is shown by the following equation.

$$AaBb \rightleftarrows aA^{+x} + bB^{-y}$$

Mathematically express the solubility product constant, $K_{sp}$, at equilibrium.

**16.** A 1 L saturated solution of AgCl is evaporated to dryness, and the residue is equivalent to $2.68 \times 10^{-5}$ mol. What is the experimental $K_{sp}$ of the silver chloride?

$$AgCl(s) \rightleftarrows Ag^+(aq) + Cl^-(aq)$$

**Concept Review** *continued*

**17.** The solubility of AgCl is 0.000 013 mol/L. Calculate the $K_{sp}$ for AgCl.

**18.** If the concentration of chloride ion remaining in solution after silver chloride has been precipitated is 0.2 M, what is the concentration of the silver ion? $K_{sp}$ of AgCl is $2.8 \times 10^{-10}$.

**19.** What is the experimental $K_{sp}$ of $CaCO_3$ if the residue after evaporation of a 1.00 L saturated solution is found to have a mass of 0.006 90 g?

$$CaCO_3(s) \rightleftarrows Ca^{2+}(aq) + CO_3^{2-}(aq)$$

**20.** For a saturated silver chromate solution, the molar concentration of $CrO_4^{2-}$ is $6.54 \times 10^{-5}$ M, and the $K_{sp}$ of $Ag_2CrO_4$ is $1.12 \times 10^{-12}$ at equilibrium. Calculate the concentration of $Ag^+$ in the solution.

$$Ag_2CrO_4(s) \rightleftarrows 2Ag^+(aq) + CrO_4^{2-}(aq)$$

Skills Worksheet

# Concept Review

## Section: Equilibrium Systems and Stress

**Answer the following item in the space provided.**

**1.** State Le Châtelier's principle.

_____

_____

**2.** Name three factors that can affect an equilibrium system.

_____

_____

**3.** Consider the following system at equilibrium, and complete the tables below, indicating the system's response to a given stress to restore equilibrium.

$$2NO_2(g) \rightleftarrows N_2O_4(g) + energy$$

| Temperature | | Results | |
|---|---|---|---|
| **Stress** | **Direction of shift** | **Increase** | **Decrease** |
| Lowering temperature | | | |
| Raising temperature | left favored | $NO_2$ | $N_2O_4$ |

| Pressure | | Results | |
|---|---|---|---|
| **Stress** | **Direction of shift** | **Increase** | **Decrease** |
| Pressure increase | right favored | $N_2O_4$ | $NO_2$ |
| Pressure decrease | | | |

| Pressure | | Results | |
|---|---|---|---|
| **Stress** | **Direction of shift** | **Increase** | **Decrease** |
| Increase $[N_2O_4]$ | left favored | $NO_2$ | $N_2O_4$ |
| Increase $[NO_2]$ | | | |
| Decrease $[N_2O_4]$ | | | |
| Decrease $[NO_2]$ | | | |

## Concept Review *continued*

**Complete each statement below by writing the correct word or words in the space provided.**

| | | | |
|---|---|---|---|
| increase | endothermic | left | increases |
| decrease | exothermic | right | decreases |

4. In general, a(n) _____ in pressure shifts a system at equilibrium in the direction that produces the smaller number of moles of gases, and a(n)

   _____ in pressure shifts it in the opposite direction.

5. Energy in the form of heat is a product of the forward _____

   reaction. Increasing the temperature _____ the amount of energy

   in the system. This drives the equilibrium to the _____, consuming some of the energy as heat added. Lowering the temperature shifts the reaction

   to the _____, replenishing some of the energy that was removed.

6. If the concentration of a reactant or product _____ in a system at equilibrium, the equilibrium shifts in the direction that produces the substance.

7. If the concentration of a reactant or product _____ in a system at equilibrium, the equilibrium shifts in the direction that consumes the substance.

**Consider the following equilibrium reaction in which an excess of Br⁻ ions is added in the form of the soluble salt NaBr.**

$$AgBr(s) \rightleftharpoons Ag^+(aq) + Br^-(aq)$$

**Complete each statement below.**

8. The excess _____ ions produces a stress on the system in equilibrium.

9. The equilibrium system adjusts to the stress by shifting to the _____.

10. $Br^-$ ions are consumed, and additional _____ is formed.

11. Each $Br^-$ ion that reacts with an _____ ion.

12. The action _____ the concentration of $Ag^+$ ions.

13. AgBr is _____ soluble in NaBr than in pure water.

14. NaBr has an ion in common with AgBr; hence the name _____.

**Answer the following item in the space provided.**

15. Describe the practical uses of Le Châtelier's principle.

   _____

   _____

Skills Worksheet

# Concept Review

## Section: What Are Acids and Bases?

**In the space provided, write the letter of the description that best matches the term or phrase.**

_____ **1.** strong acid

_____ **2.** amphoteric

_____ **3.** strong base

_____ **4.** Brønsted-Lowry acid

_____ **5.** Brønsted-Lowry base

_____ **6.** conjugate acid

_____ **7.** conjugate base

**a.** a base that forms when an acid loses a proton

**b.** a base that ionizes completely in a solvent

**c.** a substance that donates a proton to another substance

**d.** an acid that ionizes completely in a solvent

**e.** an acid that forms when a base gains a proton

**f.** a substance that has the properties of an acid and the properties of a base

**g.** a substance that accepts a proton

**Answer each of the following questions in the space provided.**

**In the following equations, identify which reactant is the Brønsted-Lowry acid and which reactant is the Brønsted-Lowry base.**

**8.** $HSO_4^-(aq) + H_2O(l) \rightleftharpoons H_3O^+(aq) + SO_4^{2-}(aq)$

    **a.** Brønsted-Lowry acid _____

    **b.** Brønsted-Lowry base _____

**9.** $H_2PO_4^-(aq) + H_2O \rightleftharpoons HPO_4^{2-}(aq) + H_3O^+(aq)$

    **a.** Brønsted-Lowry acid _____

    **b.** Brønsted-Lowry base _____

**In the following equations, indicate whether amphoteric $Al(OH)_3$ is acting as an acid or as a base.**

**10.** $Al(OH)_3(s) + H_3O^+(aq) \rightarrow Al(OH)_2^+(aq) + 2H_2O(l)$ _____

**11.** $Al(OH)_3(s) + OH^-(aq) \rightarrow Al(OH)_4^-(aq)$ _____

**In the following equations, identify the conjugate acid and conjugate base in the products formed.**

12. $H_2SO_4(aq) + H_2O(l) \rightleftharpoons H_3O^+(aq) + HSO_4^-(aq)$

   **a.** conjugate acid _____

   **b.** conjugate base _____

13. $NH_4^+(aq) + OH^-(aq) \rightleftharpoons NH_3(aq) + H_2O(l)$

   **a.** conjugate acid _____

   **b.** conjugate base _____

**In the space provided, write the letter of the term or phrase that best completes each statement or best answers each question.**

_____ **14.** Which of the following is *not* a distinctive property of acids?
   **a.** conducts electricity    **c.** generates $H_3O^+$
   **b.** reacts with many metals    **d.** generates $OH^-$

_____ **15.** The Arrhenius definitions of acids and bases apply only to
   **a.** amphoteric substances.    **c.** pure substances.
   **b.** aqueous solutions.    **d.** proton acceptors.

_____ **16.** How would you classify ammonia ($NH_3$) in the equation below?
$$NH_3(aq) + H_2O(l) \rightleftharpoons NH_4^+(aq) + OH^-(aq)$$
   **a.** as a weak acid    **c.** as a weak base
   **b.** as a strong acid    **d.** as a strong base

_____ **17.** How would you classify sodium hydroxide (NaOH) in the equation below?
$$NaOH(s) \rightarrow Na^+(aq) + OH^-(aq)$$
   **a.** as a weak acid    **c.** as a weak base
   **b.** as a strong acid    **d.** as a strong base

_____ **18.** Which of the following is a property of bases?
   **a.** generates $H^+$    **c.** generates $H_3O^+$
   **b.** generates $OH^-$    **d.** all of the above

_____ **19.** How would you classify nitric acid ($HNO_3$) in the equation below?
$$HNO_3(l) + H_2O(l) \rightarrow H_3O^+(aq) + NO_3^-(aq)$$
   **a.** as a weak acid    **c.** as a weak base
   **b.** as a strong acid    **d.** as a strong base

Skills Worksheet

# Concept Review

## Section: Acidity, Basicity, and pH

**Complete each statement below by choosing a term or formula from the following list. Use each term only once.**

| | | | |
|---|---|---|---|
| $H_3O^+$ | equal | $[H_3O^+]$ | acid |
| $OH^-$ | concentration | $[OH^-]$ | system |
| constant | equilibrium | base | |
| ion product of water | $1.00 \times 10^{-14}$ | | |

**1.** The self-ionization of pure water at 25°C is a(n)_____

system in which _____ amounts of

_____ ions and _____ ions are

produced. Therefore, the _____ of these ions in pure

water must be equal.

**2.** The equilibrium _____, $K_w$, is called the

_____. In the self-ionization of water and in any

_____ involving _____ and

_____ solutions, the product of _____

and _____ must equal _____.

**Complete the statements in items 3 and 4 by referring to Table 1 below and choosing a term from the list that follows. Use each term only once.**

**TABLE 1  RELATIONSHIP BETWEEN [H⁺] AND pH IN AQUEOUS SOLUTIONS**

| | No. 1 | No. 2 | No. 3 | No. 4 | No. 5 | No. 6 | No. 7 | No. 8 | No. 9 |
|---|---|---|---|---|---|---|---|---|---|
| **[H⁺]** | $10^0$ | $10^{-2}$ | $10^{-4}$ | $10^{-6}$ | $10^{-7}$ | $10^{-8}$ | $10^{-10}$ | $10^{-12}$ | $10^{-14}$ |
| **pH** | 0 | 2 | 4 | 6 | 7 | 8 | 10 | 12 | 14 |

|  Acidic  |  Neutral  |  Basic  |

| | | | | |
|---|---|---|---|---|
| higher | inversely | increases | 10 | 3 |
| decreases | lower | hydronium ion | pH | |

**3. Table 1** shows that $[H_3O^+]$ and pH are _____ related. As $[H_3O^+]$

decreases from $10^{-8}$ M to $10^{-10}$ M, pH _____ from 8 to 10. In

general, as the _____ concentration decreases, the

_____ increases. In other words, the _____ the pH, the

less acidic (more basic) the solution.

**4.** A solution of pH 6 has a(n) _____ $[H_3O^+]$ than does a

solution of pH 4. When pH increases by one unit, $[H_3O^+]$

_____ by a factor of _____. A solution

of pH _____ has a $[H_3O^+]$ one-tenth that of a solution of

pH 2 and 10 times that of a solution of pH 4.

**Answer each of the following questions in the space provided.**

**5.** Explain how a mixture of indicators, like those in pH paper, is used to determine pH.

_____

_____

**6.** Describe a pH meter, and briefly describe how such a device measures pH.

_____

_____

_____

**Solve the following problems, and write your answer in the space provided.**

**7.** Determine the $[OH^-]$ of a solution that contains $1 \times 10^{-5}$ mol of $H_3O^+$ per
liter.

## Concept Review *continued*

**8.** What is the pH of a 0.10 M solution of HCl, a strong acid?

**9.** The $[OH^-]$ in a solution is $5 \times 10^{-5}$ M. What is the $[H_3O^+]$ and pH of this solution?

Skills Worksheet

# Concept Review

## Section: Neutralizations and Titrations

**Complete each statement below by choosing a term from the following list. Use each term only once.**

| | | | | |
|---|---|---|---|---|
| unknown | hydronium | titration | equivalence point | water |
| equivalent | standard | hydroxide | neutralization | salt |

1. A _____ is an experimental procedure in which a solution

of accurately known concentration, a(n) _____ solution,

is added slowly to a solution of _____ concentration until

the chemical reaction between the two solutions is complete. The most

common titration involves the reaction of an acidic solution with a basic

solution and is called a(n) _____. The products of this

reaction are a(n) _____ and _____.

2. In theory, during the titration of a strong acid with a strong base, the standard

base is added until the amount of base is chemically

_____ to the amount of acid in the unknown sample. At

this point, called the_____, the number of

_____ ions from the added base solution equals the

number of _____ ions furnished by the acid solution.

**In the blank at the left of each of the following state-
ments, write the letter from Figure 1 that best matches
that statement.**

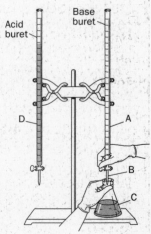

Acid buret

Base buret

D

A

B

C

_____ **3.** Used to deliver and measure the volume of the
acid added to the titration flask

_____ **4.** Used to deliver and measure the volume of the
titrant needed

_____ **5.** Used to regulate the flow of standard solution

_____ **6.** Used to hold an unknown quantity of acid and
an indicator

## Concept Review *continued*

**Use Figures 2 and 3 below to answer the following items.**

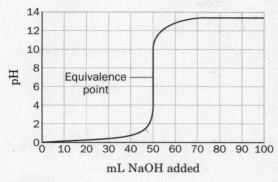

**Figure 2**

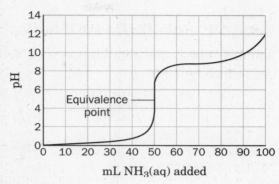

**Figure 3**

7. The titration curve for a neutralization reaction is shown in **Figure 2**. The pH

   at the end point is _____. The indicator selected should

   change color in the pH range from about _____ to

   _____. One indicator that meets this criterion is

   _____.

8. The titration curve for a strong acid/weak base titration is shown in **Figure 3**.

   The pH at the end point is less than _____. Because of the

   low pH region in which it changes color, _____ would be a

   good indicator.

**Solve the following problem, and write your answer in the space provided.**

9. A student titrates a 4.00 mL sample of Brand X vinegar with a 0.100 M NaOH
   solution. The average volume of base solution needed to reach the equiva-
   lence point is 13.6 mL.

   **a.** What is the molarity of acetic acid in the Brand X vinegar?

   **b.** By law, vinegar must contain at least 4% acetic acid, which corresponds to
   0.67 M acetic acid. Does the concentration of acetic acid in Brand X vinegar
   meet the legal standard?

Skills Worksheet

# Concept Review

## Section: Equilibria of Weak Acids and Bases

**Refer to Table 7, Relative Strengths of Acids and Bases, in your textbook to answer the following items.**

1. The weakest acid is _____.

2. The strongest base is _____.

3. The bases that are also conjugate acids are _____.

4. Of $NH_3$ and $HCOO^-$, the weaker base is _____.

5. Of $NH_4^+$ and $HCOOH$, the weaker acid is _____.

6. Of $NH_4^+$ and $HOCl$, the weaker acid is _____.

7. Of $HCOO^-$ and $ClO^-$, the stronger base is _____.

8. Of $HOCl$ and $HCOOH$, the stronger acid is _____.

9. What happens to $K_a$ with increasing acid strength? _____

_____

10. What happens to $K_a$ with increasing base strength? _____

_____

**Complete each statement below by underlining the correct word or phrase in brackets.**

11. In an acid-base reaction, the conjugate base of the [stronger, weaker] acid is the weaker base, and the conjugate acid of the [stronger, weaker] base is the weaker acid.

12. The [higher, lower] the $K_a$ of an acid, the weaker the conjugate base; and the [higher, lower] the $K_a$ of an acid, the stronger the conjugate base.

**Solve the following problems, and write your answer in the space provided.**

13. Calculate $K_a$ for 0.100 M acetic acid at 25°C. Its $[H_3O^+]$ is $1.3 \times 10^{-3}$ mol/L.

# Concept Review continued

**14.** Calculate $K_a$ for 0.50 M HCN at 25°C. Its $[H_3O^+]$ is $1.4 \times 10^{-5}$ mol/L.

**Complete each statement below by underlining the correct word or phrase in brackets.**

**15.** A [buffer, acid] solution is made from a weak [acid, base] and its conjugate [acid, base] that neutralizes small amounts of acids and bases added to it. It is not necessary that they be present in equal amounts.

**16.** If a [acid, base] is added to a buffer solution, it will react with $H_3O^+$ removing $[H_3O^+, OH^-]$ from solution. According to [Le Châtelier's, Avogadro's] principle, the equilibrium will adjust by shifting to the right to make more $[H_3O^+, OH^-]$. This prevents the pH from changing very much.

**17.** A [buffer, acid] is most efficient when its two components have [equal, unequal] concentrations, but this is not required for a buffer to work.

Skills Worksheet

# Concept Review

## Section: What Affects the Rate of a Reaction?

**Complete each statement below by choosing a term from the following list. Use each term only once.**

| | | | | |
|---|---|---|---|---|
| time | chemical kinetics | volume | acidity | appearance |
| mass | decrease | positive | disappearance | reaction rate |

1. _____ is the decrease in reactant concentration or increase in product concentration per unit of time as a reaction proceeds.

2. The study of reaction rates, called _____, is one of the frontiers of chemistry that provides an almost unlimited supply of opportunities for chemical research.

3. Reaction rates can be noted and evaluated from the _____ of a

   reactant or the _____ of a product per unit of _____.

4. Three properties can be used to monitor the reaction rate in the following chemical reaction:

   $$Mg(s) + 2H_3O^+(aq) + 2Cl^-(aq) \rightarrow Mg^{2+}(aq) + 2Cl^-(aq) + H_2(g) + 2H_2O(l)$$

   the _____ in _____ of solid Mg; the decrease in _____, $H_3O^+$ ions, of the solution; and the _____ of $H_2$ formed, all per unit of time.

5. The minus sign in the reaction-rate equation makes the decrease in reactant

   concentration a _____ number.

6. Write the reaction-rate equation for the chemical reaction in item 4.

   _____

7. Refer back to the chemical reaction in item 4. If 0.048 g of magnesium completely reacts in 20 seconds, what is the average reaction rate in mol/s over that time interval?

   _____

| Concept Review *continued*

**In each blank next to the descriptions below, write the letter of the factor affecting the rate of reaction.**

**a.** temperature      **c.** nature of reactants

**b.** concentration      **d.** surface area

_____ **8.** A piece of steel wool heated in air (20% oxygen by volume) burns slowly, but when heated in pure oxygen, it undergoes rapid combustion, as evidenced by a dazzling shower of sparks.

_____ **9.** Storing foods and milk in a refrigerator helps to slow down reactions that ordinarily result in spoilage and souring.

_____ **10.** Powdered iron in melted sulfur reacts more rapidly than a lump of iron in melted sulfur.

_____ **11.** When a piece of magnesium ribbon is placed in a beaker of dilute hydrochloric acid, a rapid evolution of hydrogen gas occurs; when a piece of iron is placed in the same acid, hydrogen gas is evolved slowly, and the iron disappears at a relatively slow rate.

_____ **12.** Pressure cookers are used so that the reactions involved in cooking food will take place at a faster rate.

**Write your answer to the following questions in the space provided.**

**13.** If the concentrations of the products in a reaction are increasing would the signs of their rate expressions be positive or negative?

_____

_____

**14.** During a given chemical reaction explain how the following conditions may affect the reaction rate in all states of matter.

**a.** concentration

_____

_____

**b.** pressure

_____

_____

**c.** temperature

_____

_____

**Concept Review** *continued*

**15.** How does surface area affect reaction rates? Explain your answer.

_____

_____

_____

_____

**Solve the following problems, and write your answer in the space provided. Refer to Table 1 (Concentration Data and Calculations for the Decomposition of $N_2O_5$) for concentration data.**

**16.** Calculate the reaction rate of the decomposition of $N_2O_5$ between the time intervals of 40.0 to 60.0 seconds.

**17.** Calculate the reaction rate of the decomposition of $N_2O_5$ between the time intervals of 20.0 to 40.0 seconds.

Skills Worksheet

# Concept Review

## Section: How Can Reaction Rates Be Explained?

**Refer to the following reaction and rate law expressions, and use their symbols and chemical principles to complete items 1–9.**

A general reaction between A and B is represented by the following:

$$aA + bB \rightarrow cC + dD$$

Its rate law expression is as follows:

$$\text{rate} \propto [A]^n [B]^m$$

or

$$\text{rate} = k[A]^n [B]^m$$

**1.** The symbol _____ means that the rate of a chemical reaction is proportional to the product of the concentrations of the reactants.

**2.** A constant of proportionality known as the rate constant is _____.

**3.** The molar concentrations of A and B are represented by _____

and _____.

**4.** The powers to which the concentrations must be raised are _____

and _____.

**5.** The only valid way to obtain _____ and _____ is to use experimental data.

**6.** The value of _____ is the order with respect to reactant A.

**7.** The value of $m$ is the order with respect to reactant _____.

**8.** The exponents _____ and _____ may be zero, a fraction, or an integer.

**9.** The overall order of reaction is equal to the sum of _____ and

_____.

**10.** What is the order of the following reactions with the given rate law expressions?

_____ **a.** rate $= k[N_2O_5]$         _____ **c.** rate $= k[O_3][NO]$

_____ **b.** rate $= k[A]^{1/2}[B]$        _____ **d.** rate $= k[A][B]^2$

**11.** We know that the rate expression for the following reaction is

$$A_2 + 2B \rightarrow 2AB \qquad \text{rate} = k[A_2][B]^0$$

According to this rate expression, if during a reaction the concentrations of

both A and B are suddenly doubled, the reaction rate will _____

by a factor of _____.

**12.** We know that the rate expression for the following reaction is

$$2C + D_2 \rightarrow 2CD \qquad \text{rate} = k[C][D_2]^2$$

According to this rate expression, if during a reaction the concentrations of

both C and D are suddenly tripled, the reaction rate will _____ by

a factor of _____.

**13.** We know that the rate expression for the following reaction is

$$2NO + O_2 \rightarrow 2NO_2 \qquad \text{rate} = k[NO]^2[O_2]$$

Two experiments involving this reaction are carried out at the same
temperature. If during the second experiment the initial concentration of NO
is doubled, the initial concentration of $O_2$ must be multiplied by a factor of

_____ for the reaction rate to stay the same. The overall reaction

order is _____.

**14.** Explain why the energy and orientation of the collision of atoms and molecules
is important in chemical reactions.

_____

_____

_____

**15.** Determine the rate-law equation for the following reaction, given the
experimental data shown below.

$$2AB \rightarrow A_2 + 2B$$

| Trial run | [AB] | Reaction rate |
|-----------|------|---------------|
| 1 | 2.0 M | 0.25 M/s |
| 2 | 4.0 M | 0.50 M/s |

**16.** Determine the rate law equation for the following reaction, given the experimental data shown below:

$$3B \rightarrow C$$

| Trial run | [B] | Reaction rate |
|---|---|---|
| 1 | 0.4 M | 2.0 M/s |
| 2 | 0.8 M | 8.0 M/s |

**17.** Determine the rate law equation for the following reaction, given the experimental data shown below.

$$A_2 + 2B \rightarrow 2AB \qquad rate = k[B]^n[A_2]^m$$

| Trial run | [A$_2$] | [B] | Reaction rate |
|---|---|---|---|
| 1 | 1.0 M | 1.0 M | 4.0 M/s |
| 2 | 1.0 M | 2.0 M | 4.0 M/s |
| 3 | 2.0 M | 3.0 M | 8.0 M/s |

**18.** Determine the overall balanced equation for a reaction having the following proposed mechanism:

Step 1: $2NO + H_2 \rightarrow N_2 + H_2O_2$ slow

Step 2: $H_2 + H_2O_2 \rightarrow 2H_2O$ fast

**19.** What is the rate-determining step in item 18?

_____

**Concept Review** *continued*

**20**. Suggest a mechanism for the decomposition of ozone ($O_3$) into oxygen ($O_2$). This reaction takes place in two steps.

Step 1 _____

Step 2 _____

**Refer to Figure 1 to answer questions 22–26.**

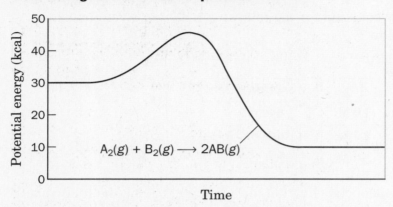

Examine the potential energy changes taking place when diatomic molecules $A_2$ react with molecules $B_2$ and form AB. The reaction's general equation is

$$A_2(g) + B_2(g) \rightarrow 2AB(g)$$

**21**. What is the activation energy, $E_a$, needed for the reaction to proceed in the forward direction?

**22**. What is the activation energy, $E_a$, needed for the reaction to proceed in the reverse direction?

**23**. Label the location of the activated complex on the curve.

**24**. The forward reaction is _____ thermic.

**25**. The reverse reaction is _____ thermic.

| Concept Review *continued*

**Choose the statement from Column B that best matches the term in Column A, and write the corresponding letter in the space provided.**

**Column A**                                    **Column B**

_____ **26.** catalysts          **a.** substances that affect reaction rates without being consumed by the overall reaction

_____ **27.** catalysis          **b.** the process by which reaction rates are increased by the addition of a catalyst

_____ **28.** enzymes            **c.** a sugar found in many dairy products

_____ **29.** lactose            **d.** a digestive enzyme that breaks down lactose

_____ **30.** lactose intolerance   **e.** nature's catalysts

_____ **31.** lactase            **f.** a condition in which a person loses the ability to produce lactase; symptoms can include painful cramps or diarrhea after eating foods with lactose

**Complete each statement below by choosing a term from the following list.**

catalytic converter    lower activation energy    regenerated    accelerate

**32.** A device used to convert harmful combustion products from automobile

exhaust to safer products is a(n) _____.

**33.** Catalyzed pathways have _____ barriers, and the catalysts

_____ the rate of the reaction.

**34.** In all catalytic pathways, the catalyst is _____.

Skills Worksheet

# Concept Review

## Section: Oxidation-Reduction Reactions

**Choose the statement from Column B that best matches the term in Column A, and write the corresponding letter in the space provided.**

**Column A**

_____ **1.** reduction

_____ **2.** oxidation

_____ **3.** redox reaction

_____ **4.** oxidation number

_____ **5.** reducing agent

_____ **6.** half-reaction

_____ **7.** oxidizing agent

**Column B**

**a.** a chemical reaction in which a substance gains electrons

**b.** any chemical process in which electrons are transferred from one substance to another

**c.** a chemical reaction in which a substance loses electrons

**d.** substance that causes reduction to happen and is itself oxidized

**e.** number assigned to an atom in a poly-atomic ion or molecular compound based on the assumption of complete transfer of electrons

**f.** substance that causes the oxidation of other substances and is itself reduced

**g.** the part of a reaction that involves only oxidation or reduction

**Determine the oxidation number for each atom in the following chemical formulas.**

**8.** $ZnCl_2$

**9.** $SO_3$

**10.** $HNO_3$

**11.** $Al_2(SO_4)_3$

**12.** $PbO$

| **Concept Review** *continued*

**13.** $CO_2$

**14.** $H_2SO_4$

**15.** Write the half-reaction for the conversion of hydrogen peroxide to water.

**16.** Identify which of the following reactions is a reduction reaction and which is an oxidation reaction. Write the balanced overall ionic equation for the redox reaction between these two.

$$Mg \rightarrow Mg^{2+} + 2e^-$$

$$O_2 + 4e^- \rightarrow 2O^{2-}$$

**Balance the following equations using the half-reaction method.**

**17.** $MnO_2^- + SO_2 \rightarrow SO_4^{2-} + Mn^{2+}$ (in acidic solution)

**18.** $NO_3^- + Cu \rightarrow NO + Cu^{2+}$ (in acidic solution)

**19.** $H_2S + NO_3^- \rightarrow NO_2 + S_8$ (in acidic solution)

**20.** In this equation identify which atoms where reduced and which were oxidized.

$$2K(s) + Cl_2(g) \rightarrow 2KCl(s)$$

_____

_____

Skills Worksheet

# Concept Review

## Section: Introduction to Electrochemistry

**Complete the following statements by choosing a term from the following list. Use each term only once.**

electric current     voltage     electrochemical cell     electrode     amperes

1. The _____ of a cell is a measure of its ability to do electrical work.

2. The movement of electrons or other charged particles is described as

   _____, and is expressed in units of _____.

3. A(n) _____ is a conductor that connects with a nonmetallic part of a circuit.

4. A(n) _____ consists of two electrodes separated by an electrolyte.

**Choose the statement from Column B that best matches the term in Column A, and write the corresponding letter in the space provided.**

**Column A**

_____ 5. electrolytes

_____ 6. metals

_____ 7. electrode

_____ 8. cathode

_____ 9. electrode reactions

_____ 10. anode

_____ 11. cathodic reaction

_____ 12. anodic reaction

**Column B**

**a.** the electrode at which oxidation takes place

**b.** conductors in which electrons carry charges

**c.** conductors in which ions in solution carry charges

**d.** the electrode at which reduction takes place

**e.** a conductor in electrical contact with an electrolyte solution

**f.** reactions that involve the transfer of electrons at the electrodes of a cell

**g.** a reaction in which electrons are released at the anode

**h.** a reaction in which electrons are consumed at the cathode

| Concept Review *continued*

**Complete each statement below by writing the correct term or phrase.**

**13.** An anode must be paired with a _____ for a redox reaction to occur.

**14.** The simplest electrochemical cell consists of two pieces of metal in an

_____ solution.

**15.** The anode is wherever _____ is going on.

**16.** A cathode is wherever _____ is going on.

**17.** In an electrochemical cell, a _____ keeps electrolyte solutions from mixing, but lets ions move.

**Solve the following problems, and write your answers in the space provided.**

**18.** Explain how electrons move between the negative and positive terminals in a typical flashlight battery.

_____

_____

_____

**19.** Write an electrode reaction in which you change $Zn(s)$ to $Zn^{+2}(aq)$. Would this reaction happen at an anode or a cathode?

**20**. Write an electrode reaction which would occur at a cathode and which involves $Cu^{2+}$. Is this reaction oxidation or reduction?

Skills Worksheet

# Concept Review

## Section: Galvanic Cells

**Complete each statement by underlining the correct word in brackets.**

1. In concept, fuel cells are very [simple, complex].

2. The fuel cell in your text shows that the fuel and oxidizer are supplied to [two, four] electrodes from [outside, within] the cell. The [two, four] electrodes are separated by a [thick, thin] layer of electrolyte.

3. In conventional power plants, chemical energy in fuel is [directly, indirectly] turned into electrical energy; the process is [efficient, inefficient].

4. The fuel cell [directly, indirectly] converts chemical energy into electrical energy; the process is [simple, difficult] and [efficient, inefficient].

5. Perfectly efficient energy conversion is theoretically [possible, impossible] with fuel cells.

6. Batteries are self-contained [galvanic, electrolytic] cells.

7. Batteries convert [electrical, chemical] energy into [electrical, chemical] energy.

8. The battery is a [fixed, portable] means of energy.

9. The common zinc-carbon battery is a(n) [acidic, alkaline] cell.

10. The [alkaline, lead-acid] cell is a newer, better version of the acidic cell.

11. Dry cells are not dry; a [carbon, zinc] rod, the battery's positive terminal, contacts a wet paste.

12. The batteries in electronic devices around your home are probably [acidic, alkaline] cells.

13. A [steel, paper] outer shell is needed to prevent caustic contents from leaking out of an alkaline cell.

14. The standard automobile battery is a [lead-, zinc-] acid storage cell.

15. [Lead(II) sulfate, copper(II) sulfate] is produced at both electrodes in an automobile battery.

16. When an automobile battery discharges, it acts as a [galvanic, electrolytic] cell; when it recharges, it functions as an [galvanic, electrolytic] cell.

17. The energy to drive the [recharging, discharging] of an automobile battery comes from an internal source, such as the car's engine.

18. [Galvanic, Electrolytic] cells generate electrical energy.

19. A [Daniell, Downs] cell converts chemical energy into electrical energy.

**Concept Review** *continued*

## Solve the following problems, and write your answers in the space provided.

**20.** Calculate the voltage of a cell for the reaction between a silver electrode in a solution containing silver ions and a zinc electrode in a solution containing zinc ions. Identify the anode and the cathode.

**21.** Calculate the voltage of a cell for the reaction between a copper electrode in a solution containing copper(II) ions and a lead electrode in a solution containing lead(II) ions. Identify the anode and the cathode.

**22.** Write the electrochemical equation for the reaction that will naturally occur in a cell that contains a zinc, $Zn^{2+}/Zn$, electrode and a copper, $Cu^{2+}/Cu$, electrode.

**23.** Write the electrochemical equation for the reaction that will naturally occur in a cell that contains a chlorine, $Cl_2$, electrode and an iodine, $I_2$, electrode.

**24.** Write the electrochemical equation for the reaction that will naturally occur in a cell that contains a silver, $Ag^+/Ag$, electrode and a copper, $Cu^{2+}/Cu$, electrode.

**Concept Review** *continued*

**Answer the following items in the space provided.**

**25.** Define *corrosion*.

_____

_____

_____

**26.** List the three ingredients generally required in the corrosion of metals.

_____

_____

_____

**27.** Explain why corrosion is more likely to occur when two different metals are in contact with one another. Give an example.

_____

_____

_____

_____

**28.** Describe cathodic protection.

_____

_____

_____

_____

_____

_____

Skills Worksheet

# Concept Review

## Section: Electrolytic Cells

**For questions 1–8, complete each statement below by referring to Figure 1 and choosing a term from the following list. Use each term only once.**

**Figure 1**

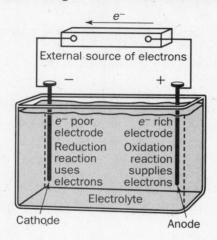

| cathode | electrolysis | negative | released | Downs cell | reduction |
|---|---|---|---|---|---|
| anode | electrosynthesis | electrolytic | positive | Downs | |
| nonspontaneous | electrical | oxidation | consumed | molten | |

1. _____ cells are electrochemical cells in which _____ chemical reactions are made to occur by an external source of _____ energy.

2. Sodium is manufactured by the _____ of _____ sodium chloride. This method is named the _____ process and is carried out industrially in an electrolytic cell, the _____.

3. Electrons are _____ at the anode (_____) and _____ at the cathode (_____); therefore, electrons travel through the wire from _____ to _____.

4. Since the reaction is nonspontaneous, the external power source forces electrons to flow from the _____ electrode (anode) to the _____ electrode (cathode), as in all electrolytic cells.

5. The _____ of sodium uses electrical energy.

| Concept Review *continued*

**Answer the following items in the space provided.**

6. The equation for the cathodic reaction is _____.

7. The equation for the anodic reaction is _____.

8. The equation for the net reaction is _____.

**Complete each statement below by writing the correct term or phrase.**

9. _____ occurs at the cathode during the electrolysis of water.

10. The _____ is the positive electrode in the electrolysis of water.

11. In the electrolysis of water, _____ is produced at the anode and

_____ at the cathode.

12. An _____ is added to water to make it an effective conductor
during electrolysis, but the electrolyte does not undergo any redox reactions.

13. Electrolytic cells are used to _____ metals.

14. Electrolytic cells convert _____ energy into _____
energy by using an external power source.

**Choose the statement from Column B that best matches the term in Column A, and write the corresponding letter in the space provided.**

**Column A**

_____15. bauxite

_____16. Hall-Héroult

_____17. 5%

_____18. molten cryolite

_____19. carbon-lined tank

_____20. carbon rods

_____21. 95%

_____22. electroplating

**Column B**

a. function as anodes in the Hall-Héroult process

b. name given to the electrochemical process of obtaining aluminum from its ore

c. serves as the cathode in the Hall-Héroult process

d. ore of aluminum

e. an electrochemical process in which a metal ion is reduced and a solid metal is deposited on a surface

f. percentage of electrical energy consumed in the United States to produce aluminum

g. the percentage of the cost that can be saved by recycling aluminum cans as opposed to producing aluminum cans from bauxite ore

h. $Na_3AlF_6$; used to dissolve alumina at 970°C

# Concept Review

## Section: Atomic Nuclei and Nuclear Stability

**Answer the following questions in the space provided.**

1. What is a nucleon?

_____

_____

2. What is a nuclide?

_____

_____

3. Describe how the strong force attracts nucleons.

_____

_____

_____

_____

4. What is nuclear binding energy?

_____

_____

_____

_____

5. How is nuclear binding energy related to the mass defect?

_____

_____

_____

_____

_____

**In the blanks at the left, write the letter of the choice that best completes the statement or answers the question.**

_____ **6.** What is another name for the nucleus of an atom?
  **a.** isotope
  **b.** mass number
  **c.** nucleon
  **d.** nuclide

_____ **7.** These are atoms that have the same atomic number but different **mass** numbers.
  **a.** isotopes
  **b.** nuclei
  **c.** nucleons
  **d.** nuclides

_____ **8.** Which of the following does NOT represent an isotope of tellurium?
  **a.** $^{122}_{52}\text{Te}$
  **b.** $^{124}_{52}\text{Te}$
  **c.** $^{128}_{52}\text{Te}$
  **d.** $^{124}_{53}\text{Te}$

_____ **9.** What is the force of attraction among the particles in a nucleus that overcomes electrostatic repulsion and holds the nucleus together?
  **a.** electrostatic force
  **b.** strong force
  **c.** electromagnetic force
  **d.** nuclear binding force

_____ **10.** Which of the following does not occur when separated nucleons come together to form a nucleus?
  **a.** the release of energy
  **b.** instability of the nucleus
  **c.** increased stability of the nucleus
  **d.** a mass defect

**Concept Review** *continued*

**Complete each statement below by choosing a term from the following list. You will not use every term.**

| | | | | |
|---|---|---|---|---|
| decrease | per nucleon | less | large | mole |
| nucleus | maximum | highest | separate | stable |
| protons | mass | $^{24}_{12}Mg$ | repulsions | mass number |
| increase | mass defect | attraction | $^{56}_{26}Fe$ | nuclear binding |

**11.** The _____ represents the amount of _____ converted

into energy and released when a _____ is formed from protons and

neutrons. Specifically, if one _____ of $^{16}_{8}O$ nuclei were to be formed

from 8 mol of protons and 8 mol of neutrons, the resulting 1 mol of nuclei

would have a mass that is 0.137005 g _____ than that of the original

_____ and neutrons. Stated differently, the _____

energy for $^{16}_{8}O$ is the amount of energy required to _____ 1 mol of

$^{16}_{8}O$ nuclei into 8 mol of protons and 8 mol of neutrons.

**12.** Consider a graph that plots average binding energy per nucleon versus mass

number. This graph shows that nuclear binding energies _____

rapidly with increasing mass number, reach a _____ around mass

number 55, and then slowly _____. The nuclei with the

_____ binding energies (mass numbers 40 to 150) are the most

stable. Beyond these elements, the nucleus is too _____ for added

nucleons to increase the overall _____ among the particles, and

_____ become more significant. Stated differently, isotopes that

have a high binding energy per nucleon are more _____. The most

stable nucleus is _____.

**Concept Review** *continued*

**Complete each statement below by writing the correct term in the space provided.**

**13.** Because a strong force of attraction holds nuclear particles together, a

nucleus is at a _____ energy state than are its separated nucleons.

**14.** The energy produced during the formation of a nucleus is very

_____ compared with the energy changes that take place in ordinary chemical reactions.

**15.** During the formation of a nucleus, energy is produced at the expense of

_____

**Refer to the rules for predicting nuclear stability. Complete each statement by underlining the correct word in brackets.**

**16.** All 256 of the known stable nuclei, represented by red dots, form a pattern called the band of [stability, nuclear bonding].

**17.** Above atomic number 20, the most stable nuclides have [more, fewer] neutrons than protons.

**18.** Except for the smallest nuclei, all stable nuclei contain a number of neutrons that is [less than or equal to, equal to or greater] than the number of protons.

**19.** Almost [60%, 90%] of all stable nuclei have even numbers of protons and neutrons.

**20.** Nuclei with even numbers of protons and neutrons (an even-even combination) are particularly [unstable, stable].

**21.** $^{16}_{8}O$, $^{40}_{20}Ca$, and $^{88}_{38}Sr$ are nuclei with so-called magic numbers of nucleons and tend to be very [unstable, stable].

Skills Worksheet )

# Concept Review

## Section: Nuclear Change

**Answer the following questions in the space provided.**

1. What is radioactivity?

   _____

   _____

2. Describe what happens when a nucleus is stabilized by converting neutrons into protons.

   _____

   _____

   _____

   _____

3. Describe what happens when a nucleus is stabilized by converting protons into neutrons.

   _____

   _____

   _____

   _____

4. Describe what happens when a nucleus is stabilized by emitting positrons.

   _____

   _____

   _____

   _____

5. Describe what happens when a nucleus is stabilized by losing alpha particles.

   _____

   _____

   _____

   _____

**6.** Complete the following table about different types of radioactive decay.

| Type of Radioactive Decay | What happens to the atomic number? | What happens to the mass number? |
|---|---|---|
| Beta-particle emission | | |
| electron capture | | |
| positron emission | | |
| alpha particle emission | | |

**Write balanced nuclear equations for the following, and name the type of radioactive emission formed when each occurs.**

**7.** $^{51}_{24}Cr + ^{0}_{-1}e \rightarrow$ _____ $+ \gamma$      emission: _____

**8.** $^{226}_{88}Ra \rightarrow$ _____ $+ ^{4}_{2}He$      emission: _____

**9.** $^{239}_{93}Np \rightarrow$ _____ $+ ^{0}_{+1}e$      emission: _____

**10.** $^{234}_{91}Pa \rightarrow$ _____ $+ ^{0}_{-1}e$      emission: _____

**11.** $^{49}_{24}Cr \rightarrow ^{49}_{23}V +$ _____      emission: _____

**12.** $^{238}_{92}U \rightarrow ^{234}_{90}Th +$ _____      emission: _____

**13.** $^{214}_{83}Bi \rightarrow ^{214}_{84}Po +$ _____      emission: _____

**Categorize each nuclear equation below by writing the correct term from the following list. Terms may be used more than once.**

beta particle emission      electron capture      positron emission

alpha particle emission      annihilation of matter

**14.** $^{0}_{-1}e + ^{0}_{+1}e \rightarrow 2\gamma$      type: _____

**15.** $^{1}_{1}p \rightarrow ^{1}_{0}n + ^{0}_{+1}e$      type: _____

**16.** $^{37}_{18}Ar + ^{0}_{-1}e \rightarrow ^{37}_{17}Cl + \gamma$      type: _____

**17.** $^{238}_{92}U \rightarrow ^{234}_{90}Th + ^{4}_{2}He$      type: _____

**18.** $^{1}_{0}n \rightarrow ^{1}_{1}H + ^{0}_{-1}e$      type: _____

**Complete each statement below by writing the correct term in the space provided.**

**19.** Nuclei that have an excess of neutrons can become stable by emitting

_____.

**20.** Any time a particle collides with an _____, all of the mass of the two particles is converted into electromagnetic energy.

**21.** A positron colliding with an electron resulting in the release of gamma rays, this process is known as the _____.

**22.** _____ emission changes neither the atomic number nor the mass number.

**23.** In _____, a proton is changed into a neutron.

**24.** In beta emission, an electron is emitted by a _____.

**25.** None of the elements above atomic number 83 and mass number 126 have stable isotopes, and many stabilize by _____.

**26.** A few sheets of paper can stop _____.

**27.** In an alpha emission, the atomic number of the nucleus decreases by _____ while the mass number decreases by _____.

**Complete each statement below by choosing a term from the following list. Use each term only once.**

fission      fusion      sustains      chain reaction      fuse
neutrons      binding energy      spontaneous      critical mass

**28.** Nuclear _____ refers to a nuclear reaction in which a very heavy nucleus splits into two smaller nuclei, each having a higher _____ per nucleon than the original nucleus. A very small fraction of naturally occurring uranium atoms undergoes _____ fission. Most fission reactions are artificially induced by bombarding nuclei with _____. A _____ is a fission reaction which, once initiated, _____ itself. The smallest mass of radioactive material needed to sustain a chain reaction is known as the _____ of the material.

## Concept Review *continued*

**29.** Nuclear _____ occurs when two small nuclei combine, or

_____, to form a larger, more stable nucleus with a higher binding

energy.

**Categorize each nuclear equation below as *fission* or *fusion*.**

**30.** $^3_1\text{H} + {}^2_1\text{H} \rightarrow {}^4_2\text{He} + {}^1_0 n$        type: _____

**31.** $^{239}_{94}\text{Pu} + {}^1_0 n \rightarrow {}^{90}_{38}\text{Sr} + {}^{147}_{56}\text{Ba} + 3{}^1_0 n$        type: _____

**32.** $^{235}_{92}\text{U} \rightarrow {}^{90}_{38}\text{Sr} + {}^{144}_{58}\text{Ce} + {}^1_0 n + 4{}^{\phantom{-}0}_{-1} e$        type: _____

**33.** $2{}^3_2\text{He} \rightarrow {}^4_2\text{He} + 2{}^1_1\text{H}$        type: _____

**Answer the following items in the space provided.**

**34.** Describe potential benefits and hazards of nuclear fission.

_____

_____

_____

_____

_____

_____

_____

_____

**Concept Review** *continued*

**35.** Describe nuclear fusion and its potential as an energy source.

_____

_____

_____

_____

_____

_____

_____

_____

Skills Worksheet

# Concept Review

## Section: Uses of Nuclear Chemistry

**Answer the following in the space provided.**

1. Define half-life.

_____

_____

_____

_____

2. How can half-lives be used to determine an object's age?

_____

_____

_____

_____

_____

**In the blanks at the left, write the letter of the choice that best completes the statement or answers the question.**

_____ 3. The equation $^{40}_{19}K + ^{\ \ 0}_{-1}e \rightarrow ^{40}_{18}Ar + \gamma$ represents the decay of potassium-40 by _____ to argon-40.
   a. beta emission
   b. electron capture
   c. positron emission
   d. alpha decay

_____ 4. Potassium-40, with a half-life of _____ years, is useful in dating ancient rocks and minerals.
   a. 1.28 million
   b. 1.28 trillion
   c. 12.8 billion
   d. 1.28 billion

_____ **5.** The equation $^{14}_{6}C \rightarrow {}^{14}_{7}N + {}^{0}_{-1}e$ represents the decay of carbon-14 by
_____ to nitrogen-14.
   **a.** beta emission
   **b.** electron capture
   **c.** positron emission
   **d.** alpha decay

_____ **6.** Carbon-14, useful in dating the plants and animals of Earth's food
chain, has a half-life of how many years?
   **a.** 5715
   **b.** 571.5
   **c.** 57 150
   **d.** None of the above

_____ **7.** If an original sample of carbon-14 has a mass of 10 g, at the end of
11 430 years, the amount of carbon-14 remaining would be _____ g.
   **a.** 2.5
   **b.** 5
   **c.** 10
   **d.** 50

_____ **8.** Smoke detectors rely on _____ to ionize gas molecules, which help to
detect smoky air.
   **a.** alpha particles
   **b.** beta particles
   **c.** positrons
   **d.** gamma rays

_____ **9.** The radioactive isotope used most widely in nuclear medicine is _____.
   **a.** thallium-201
   **b.** technetium-99
   **c.** americium-241
   **d.** radon-222

_____**10.** During a PET scan, gamma rays are detected by a scanner, which con-
verts the information into _____.
   **a.** a three-dimensional picture of a person's organs
   **b.** an image of a person's heart
   **c.** a photographic image of bone repair
   **d.** None of the above

_____**11.** The identification of elements by which of the following has been put
to use in detecting art forgeries?
  **a.** carbon-14 dating
  **b.** radon-222 dating
  **c.** neutron activation analysis
  **d.** potassium-40 dating

_____**12.** People who work with radioactive isotopes are advised to limit their
exposure to how many rems per year?
  **a.** 10
  **b.** 5
  **c.** 25
  **d.** 2.5

_____**13.** A marked decrease in white-blood-cell count can result from a dose of
how many rems of radiation?
  **a.** 0–25
  **b.** 25–50
  **c.** 50–100
  **d.** more than 100

**Answer the following in the space provided.**

**14.** Compare acute and chronic exposure to radiation.

_____

_____

_____

_____

_____

**15.** What similarities do you notice about the nuclear reactions used in medicine
that are mentioned in the text?

_____

_____

_____

_____

_____

# Concept Review *continued*

**Solve the following problem, and write your answer in the spaces in the table.**

**16.** The half-life of radon-222 is approximately 4 days. If a tube containing 1.00 microgram of radon were stored in a hospital clinic for 12 days, how much radon would remain in the tube? Use the table below to determine successive half-life amounts during the 12-day period.

| Days | 0 | 4 | 8 | 12 |
|------|---|---|---|----|
| Radon remaining | | | | |

**Solve the following problems, and write your answer in the space provided.**

**17.** The half-life of iodine-131 is approximately 8 days. How much of an original sample will be left after 24 days?

**18.** Thorium-234 has a half-life of 24 days. If 1 gram remains in a sealed container after 72 days, how much was there to begin with?

**19.** You find an ancient artifact with a ratio of carbon-14 to carbon-12 that is one quarter the ratio in a similar object today. About how old is the artifact?

**20.** The half-life of polonium-218 is 3.0 minutes. What percentage of the original sample remains after 4 half-lives?

Skills Worksheet

# Concept Review

## Section: Compounds of Carbon

**Answer the following questions in the space provided.**

1. What three factors enable carbon to form an enormous number of stable carbon compounds with very different properties?

   _____

   _____

   _____

   _____

2. Describe the molecular structure of diamond.

   _____

   _____

   _____

3. Describe the structure of graphite.

   _____

   _____

   _____

   _____

4. What are some of the uses of graphite?

   _____

   _____

   _____

Name _____ Class _____ Date _____

## Concept Review *continued*

**5.** Describe two other allotropes of carbon.

_____

_____

_____

_____

_____

_____

**6.** What characteristics does carbon have that enables it to form more known compounds than all the other elements combined?

_____

_____

_____

_____

_____

_____

_____

**7.** What is a hydrocarbon?

_____

_____

**Complete each statement below by writing the correct term or phrase.**

**8.** The prefix used for naming an organic compound that has a ring structure is

_____.

**9.** Cyclobutane is the name of the ring compound with _____ carbon atoms.

**10.** _____ is an organic ring compound that is often shown having alternating single and double bonds. These bonds all have the same bond energies.

**11.** Benzene is the simplest member of a class of organic compounds called

_____ compounds.

Copyright © by Holt, Rinehart and Winston. All rights reserved.
Holt Chemistry                    163            Carbon and Organic Compounds

Name _____ Class _____ Date _____

**| Concept Review** *continued*

**Complete each statement below by choosing a term from the following list. Terms may be used more than once.**

| | | | |
|---|---|---|---|
| alkane | alkene | alkyne | isomers |
| alcohol | aldehyde | halide | amine |
| carboxylic acid | ester | ether | ketone |

**12.** A hydrocarbon that contains one or more triple bonds is an _____.

**13.** A hydrocarbon that contains only single bonds is an _____.

**14.** A compound that has the same chemical composition but a different structure from another compound is an _____.

**15.** A hydrocarbon that contains one or more double bonds is an _____.

**16.** The _____ functional group is a single-bonded OH in the structure.

**17.** The _____ functional group is an O double-bonded to a carbon and an OH single-bonded to the same carbon.

**18.** The _____ functional group is an O double-bonded to a carbon and an H single-bonded to the same carbon.

**19.** The _____ functional group is a nitrogen singly bonded to one or more carbon atoms.

**20.** The _____ functional group is simply an O double-bonded to a carbon.

**Answer the following items in the space provided.**

**21.** Why are functional groups often responsible for how an organic compound reacts?

_____

_____

_____

**22.** Explain how the structural difference between isomers is related to the difference in their properties.

_____

_____

_____

_____

_____

Skills·Worksheet )

# Concept Review

## Section: Names and Structures of Organic Compounds

**1.** Complete the table below for straight-chain hydrocarbons.

| Number of carbon atoms | Prefix |
|---|---|
| 1 | meth- |
| 2 | |
| | prop- |
| | but- |
| 5 | |
| 6 | |
| 7 | |
| 8 | |
| 9 | |
| 10 | |

**Answer the items below in the space provided.**

**2.** What is the difference between a saturated hydrocarbon and an unsaturated hydrocarbon?

_____

_____

_____

_____

_____

_____

**3.** What is the name of the following compound?

$$CH_3-CH_2-CH_2-CH_3$$

_____

**4.** What is the name of the following compound?

$$CH_2=CH-CH_3$$

_____

| Concept Review *continued*

**5.** What is the name of the compound with the formula $C_2H_2$?

_____

**Draw the structure of the following compounds.**

**6.** propyne

**7.** ethane

**8.** ethene

**9.** 1-butene

**Complete each statement below by writing the correct term from the following list.**

    -ol          -al          amino-          -one          -oic acid

**10.** If an alcohol functional group is added to an organic compound, the name of

the compound will end in _____.

**11.** If a carboxylic acid functional group is added to an organic compound, the

name of the compound will end in _____.

**12.** If a ketone functional group is added to an organic compound, the name of

the compound will end in _____.

**Concept Review** *continued*

**13.** If an aldehyde functional group is added to an organic compound, the name

of the compound will end in _____.

**14.** If an amine functional group is added to an organic compound, the name of

the compound will begin with _____.

**Answer the items below in the space provided.**

**15.** Name the organic compound below.

$$H_3C \diagdown \atop H_3C \diagup C=C \diagup H \atop \diagdown H$$

**16.** What are the structural and molecular formulas for phenol?

Skills Worksheet

# Concept Review

## Section: Organic Reactions

**Answer the following items in the space provided.**

1. What is an addition reaction?

_____

_____

_____

_____

_____

2. What is a substitution reaction?

_____

_____

_____

_____

_____

3. What is the difference between a substitution reaction and an addition reaction?

_____

_____

_____

_____

_____

4. What is a condensation reaction?

_____

_____

_____

_____

_____

## Concept Review *continued*

**5.** What is an elimination reaction?

_____

_____

_____

_____

**6.** What is the difference between a condensation reaction and an elimination reaction?

_____

_____

_____

_____

**7.** Why are catalysts often used in substitution reactions of saturated compounds?

_____

_____

_____

_____

**8.** What is hydrogenation?

_____

_____

_____

_____

9. What is the difference between an unhydrogenated oil and a hydrogenated fat?

_____

_____

_____

_____

10. What is a monomer?

_____

_____

_____

11. What is a polymer?

_____

_____

_____

_____

12. What is the difference between polyethylene and a similar polymer with an ethane side chain?

_____

_____

_____

_____

13. Describe nylon 66 and how it is formed.

_____

_____

_____

_____

_____

_____

Skills Worksheet )

# Concept Review

## Section: Carbohydrates and Lipids

**Complete each statement below by choosing a term from the following list. Terms may be used more than once.**

| | | | |
|---|---|---|---|
| carbohydrate | monosaccharide | disaccharide | polysaccharide |
| condensation | hydrolysis | lipid | sugar |
| glycogen | polymer | starch | cellulose |

**1.** A _____ is a simple sugar that is the basic sub-unit of a carbohydrate.

**2.** A _____ is a carbohydrate made up of long chains of simple sugars.

**3.** A _____ is an organic compound made of carbon, hydrogen, and oxygen that provides nutrients to the cells of living things.

**4.** A _____, such as a fat or steroid, does not dissolve in water.

**5.** The polysaccharide that plants use for storing energy is _____.

**6.** A _____ is a sugar formed from two monosaccharides.

**7.** Many animals use an energy-storage carbohydrate called _____.

**8.** The carbohydrate _____ comes from wood fiber and is the most abundant organic compound on Earth.

**9.** A monosaccharide and a disaccharide are both examples of a simple

_____.

**10.** A polysaccharide or other large, chainlike molecule found in living things is

called a biological _____.

**11.** A _____ reaction is one in which two or more molecules combine, producing water or another simple molecule in the process.

**12.** A _____ reaction is one in which the decomposition of a biological polymer takes place along with the breakdown of a water molecule.

**13.** Many monosaccharides or disaccharides can combine to form a long chain

called a _____.

**14.** Maltose and sucrose are both examples of a _____.

**15.** Fructose and glucose are examples of a _____.

| Concept Review *continued*

**16.** Chitin is a _____.

**17.** Complete the table below.

| Carbohydrate name | Structure | Role |
|---|---|---|
| starch | | |
| glycogen | polysaccharide | energy storage in animals |
| cellulose | | |
| sucrose | disaccharide | table sugar |
| glucose | | |
| fructose | monosaccharide | sugar found in fruits |
| lactose | | |
| maltose | | |
| chitin | | |
| amylose | | |

**Answer the following items in the space provided.**

**18.** Relate the structure of carbohydrates to their role in biological systems.

_____

_____

_____

_____

**19.** What is a condensation reaction?

_____

_____

_____

_____

**20.** What is a hydrolysis reaction?

_____

_____

_____

_____

# Concept Review

## Section: Proteins

**Complete each statement below by choosing a term from the following list. Terms may be used more than once.**

| | | | |
|---|---|---|---|
| protein | amino acid | polypeptide | enzyme |
| denature | disulfide | primary | secondary |
| tertiary | quaternary | pleated sheet | helix |
| active site | substrate | trypsin | peptide |

**1.** A(n) _____ is any one of twenty organic molecules that contain a carboxyl and an amino group and that combine to form proteins.

**2.** A(n) _____ is an organic compound made up of one or more chains of amino acids that is a principal component of all cells.

**3.** A(n) _____ bond is one that forms between the carboxyl group of one amino acid and the amino group of another amino acid.

**4.** A(n) _____ bridge can form a looped protein or two separate polypeptides.

**5.** Coils and folds that are often held in place by hydrogen bonds give a protein

its _____ structure.

**6.** The three-dimensional shape of a protein is its _____ structure.

**7.** The amino-acid sequence of a polypeptide chain is the _____ structure of a protein.

**8.** A(n) _____ structure arises when different polypeptide chains that have their own three-dimensional structure come together to form a larger protein.

**9.** A secondary structure called an alpha- _____ is shaped like a coil with hydrogen bonds that form along a single segment of a peptide.

**10.** A secondary structure called a beta- _____ is shaped like an accordion with hydrogen bonds that form between adjacent polypeptide segments.

**11.** Because of a difference in only one _____, the entire shape of hemoglobin is different in the blood cells of people with sickle cell anemia.

**12.** A(n) _____ is a type of protein that speeds up metabolic reactions in plants and animals without being permanently changed or destroyed.

**Concept Review** *continued*

**13.** Only a small part of an enzyme's surface, called the _____, makes an enzyme active.

**14.** Curly hair is the result of _____ bridges in hair proteins.

**15.** In reactions that use an enzyme, the reactant is called a(n) _____.

**16.** To cause a protein to lose its tertiary and quaternary structures is to

_____ it.

**17.** A protein-splitting enzyme called _____ is used in the small intestine to help break down proteins into amino acids through hydrolysis.

**Complete each item below in the space provided.**

**18.** Describe how amino acids form proteins through condensation reactions.

_____

_____

_____

_____

_____

**19.** Describe four different kinds of interactions between side chains on a polypeptide molecule that help to make the shape that a protein takes.

_____

_____

_____

_____

_____

**20.** How do enzymes work?

_____

_____

_____

_____

_____

Skills Worksheet )

# Concept Review

## Section: Nucleic Acids

**Complete each statement below by choosing a term from the following list. Terms may be used more than once.**

| | | | |
|---|---|---|---|
| nucleic acid | DNA | RNA | gene |
| clone | recombinant DNA | uracil | triplet |
| nitrogenous | genetic code | DNA fingerprint | autoradiograph |
| stem cell | PCR | deoxyribose | helix |

**1.** The material that contains the information that determines inherited

   characteristics is called _____.

**2.** The sugar in DNA is _____.

**3.** A(n) _____ is an organic compound, either RNA or DNA, whose molecules are made up of one or two chains of nucleotides that carry genetic information.

**4.** A(n) _____ is a segment of DNA in a chromosome that codes for a specific hereditary trait.

**5.** Protein synthesis begins with a cell making a(n) _____ strand that codes for a specific protein.

**6.** RNA has the base _____ instead of the base thymine found in DNA.

**7.** The _____ is a listing of the RNA triplets and their corresponding amino acids.

**8.** RNA is composed of four _____ bases.

**9.** The pattern of bands that results when a person's DNA sample is fragmented,

   replicated, and separated is called a(n) _____.

**10.** A DNA strand is often found in the form of a double _____.

**11.** Scientists use a method called _____ to replicate a short sequence of double-stranded DNA.

**12.** A(n) _____ is an organism that is produced by asexual reproduction and that is genetically identical to its parent.

**13.** A(n) _____ is an undifferentiated cell that has not yet specialized to become a specific tissue in an animal.

Name _____ Class _____ Date _____

| **Concept Review** *continued*

**14.** DNA molecules that are artificially created by combining DNA from different

sources is called _____.

**15.** Like a polysaccharide or a polypeptide, a(n) _____ is a biological polymer.

**16.** A group of three RNA bases, called a(n) _____, indicates a particular amino acid.

**17.** An image that shows the DNA's pattern of nitrogenous bases is a(n)

_____.

**18.** Nucleic acids are formed from equal numbers of three chemical units: a sugar,

a phosphate group, and a(n) _____ base.

**Answer the following items in the space provided.**

**19.** How does DNA replicate itself?

_____

_____

_____

_____

_____

_____

**20.** A segment of DNA has the base sequence TAC TTT TCG AAG AGT ATT.

**a.** What is the base sequence in a complementary strand of RNA?

_____

**b.** What is the corresponding amino acid sequence?

_____

**c.** What is the base sequence in a complementary strand of DNA?

_____

**Concept Review** *continued*

**21.** A segment of DNA has the base sequence TAC CTT ACA GAT TGT ACT.

    **a.** What is the base sequence in the complementary strand of RNA?

    _____

    **b.** What is the corresponding amino acid sequence?

    _____

    **c.** What is the base sequence in the complementary strand of DNA?

    _____

**22.** What is cloning, and how has it been accomplished in mammals?

_____

_____

_____

_____

Name _____ Class _____ Date _____

# Concept Review

## Section: Energy in Living Systems

**Complete each statement below by choosing a term from the following list. Terms may be used more than once.**

| | | | |
|---|---|---|---|
| photosynthesis | respiration | ATP | chlorophyll |
| exothermic | glycolysis | Kreb's | synthetic |
| mechanical | transport | carbon | cellular |

**1.** In the _____ cycle, reactions involving carbon compounds give plants and animals the energy they need.

**2.** Plants and animals use glucose to produce chemical energy in the form of a substance called _____.

**3.** Green plants get energy directly from the sun's rays through a process called _____.

**4.** Most plants use _____, a magnesium-containing molecule, to capture the sun's energy.

**5.** The entire process of getting oxygen into body tissues and allowing it to react with glucose to generate energy is called _____.

**6.** Chemical, or _____, respiration takes place in the cells of a plant or animal and is fueled by glucose and oxygen.

**7.** Respiration is a(n) _____ process that gives off energy.

**8.** The first stage of cellular respiration involves _____, in which a six-carbon glucose is split into two molecules.

**9.** The second stage of cellular respiration is called the _____ cycle, which forms carbon dioxide.

**10.** ATP gives the energy needed for _____ work, which allows muscles to flex and move.

**11.** ATP gives the energy needed for _____ work, which carries solutes across membranes.

**12.** ATP gives the energy needed for _____ work, which makes compounds that do not form spontaneously.

**| Concept Review** *continued*

**Answer the following items in the space provided.**

**13.** How do plants use photosynthesis to gather energy?

_____

_____

_____

_____

_____

**14.** Explain how animals indirectly gather energy from the sun.

_____

_____

_____

_____

_____

**15.** How is cellular respiration the opposite of photosynthesis?

_____

_____

_____

_____

_____

**16.** Describe the two stages of cellular respiration.

_____

_____

_____

_____

_____